PARLIAMENTS AND PRESSURE GROUPS IN WESTERN EUROPE

THE LIBRARY OF LEGISLATIVE STUDIES

General Editor
Philip Norton
ISSN 1460-9649

A series of new and recent books exploring the role of legislatures in contemporary political systems. The volumes typically draw together a team of country specialists to provide in-depth analysis.

Parliaments in Contemporary Western Europe
edited by Philip Norton

Volume 1: *Parliaments and Governments in Western Europe*
Volume 2: *Parliaments and Pressure Groups in Western Europe*
Volume 3: *Parliaments and Citizens in Western Europe*

Conscience and Parliament
edited by Philip Cowley

The New Roles of Parliamentary Committees
edited by Lawrence D. Longley and Roger H. Davidson

*Members of Parliament in Western Europe:
Roles and Behaviour*
edited by Wolfgang C. Müller and Thomas Saalfeld

Parliaments in Western Europe
edited by Philip Norton

The New Parliaments of Central and Eastern Europe
edited by David M. Olson and Philip Norton

National Parliaments and the European Union
edited by Philip Norton

PARLIAMENTS IN CONTEMPORARY
WESTERN EUROPE

Volume 2

Parliaments and Pressure Groups in Western Europe

Edited by
PHILIP NORTON

FRANK CASS
LONDON • PORTLAND, OR

First published in 1999 in Great Britain by
FRANK CASS PUBLISHERS
Newbury House, 900 Eastern Avenue,
London IG2 7HH, England

and in the United States of America by
FRANK CASS PUBLISHERS
c/o ISBS, 5804 N.E. Hassalo Street,
Portland, Oregon 97213-3644

Website http://www.frankcass.com

Copyright © 1999 Frank Cass & Co. Ltd

British Library Cataloguing in Publication Data

Parliaments in contemporary western Europe
  Vol.2: Parliaments and pressure groups in western Europe.
  – (Library of legislative studies)
  1. Legislative bodies – Europe, Western 2. Pressure groups –
  Europe, Western 3. Politics, Practical – Europe, Western
  I. Norton, Philip
  328.4

ISBN 0 7146 4834 5 (cloth)
ISBN 0 7146 4386 6 (paper)
ISSN 1460–9649

Library of Congress Cataloging-in-Publication Data

Parliaments and goverments in Western Europe / edited by Philip
Norton.
      p. cm. – (Library of legislative studies)
   Includes index.
   ISBN 0-7146-4834-5. – ISBN 0-7146-4386-6 (pbk.)
   1. Legislative bodies – Europe, Western. 2. Europe, Western –
Politics and government. I. Norton, Philip. II. Series.
JN94.A71P38   1998
   328.3'9'094–dc21   98–16206
                                                                 CIP

All rights reserved. No part of this publication may be reproduced, stored in or introduced
into a retrieval system, or transmitted in any form, or by any means, electronic, mechanical,
photocopying, recording or otherwise without the prior permission of the
publisher of this book.

Printed in Great Britain by
Antony Rowe Ltd, Chippenham, Wiltshire

Contents

Preface	vii
List of Contributors	ix
General Introduction	xi
1. Introduction: Putting Pressure on Parliaments **Philip Norton**	1
2. The United Kingdom: Parliament Under Pressure **Philip Norton**	19
3. Germany: Bundestag and Interest Groups in a 'Party Democracy' **Thomas Saalfeld**	43
4. Parliament and Pressure Groups in Italy **Vincent Della Sala**	67
5. Belgium: Insider Pressure Groups in an Outsider Parliament **Lieven de Winter**	88
6. The Netherlands: Parliamentary Parties Rival with Pressure Groups **M.P.C.M. Van Schendelen**	110
7. Parliaments and Pressure Groups: The Irish Experience of Change **Eunan O'Halpin and Eileen Connolly**	124
8. The European Parliament: Getting the House in Order **Mark P. Shephard**	145
9. Conclusion: Conflicting Pressures **Philip Norton**	167
Index	177

Preface

This volume constitutes the second in a series of three, exploring the relationship between parliaments and key bodies in the political system. The focus of this work is the relationship between parliaments and pressure groups, a relationship that remarkably has attracted little attention, especially in comparative analysis.

I am particularly grateful to the other contributors to the volume for their hard work and commitment. For most it has involved a fairly intense period of research and writing, undertaken when they had just completed their chapters for the first volume and while having to teach and meet other writing commitments.

This is another title in the growing list of books in legislative studies published by Frank Cass. Legislatures are important subjects of study and Frank Cass has been at the forefront in ensuring that the fruits of that study are made available to a much wider audience. In reaching that wider audience, my fellow contributors and I are keen to ensure that the contact is not one way, and we welcome comments and suggestions from readers.

PHILIP NORTON
Centre for Legislative Studies, University of Hull

The Contributors

Eileen Connolly is a Research Associate in Government at Dublin City University.

Vincent Della Sala is Associate Professor of Political Science at Carleton University, Ottawa.

Lieven de Winter is Lecturer in the Départment de Sciences Politiques at the Université Catholique de Louvain and in the Faculteit Sociale Witenschappen at the Katholieke Universiteit, Brussels.

Philip Norton is Professor of Government at the University of Hull.

Eunan O'Halpin is Professor of Government at Dublin City University.

Thomas Saalfeld is Lecturer in Politics at the University of Kent.

Mark Shephard is a Doctoral Candidate in the Department of Political Science at the University of Houston.

M.C.P.M. Van Schendelen is Professor of Political Science at Erasmus University, Rotterdam.

General Introduction

PHILIP NORTON

LEGISLATURES have one core defining function: that of giving assent to measures that, by virtue of that assent, are to be binding on society.[1] In practice, they have usually performed other roles as well, such as debating measures or the conduct of public affairs. They have existed for centuries. They span the globe. Most countries have one: federal states have several. Commentators throughout the twentieth century have bemoaned the 'decline' of legislatures, yet the number shows no sign of declining: if anything, the reverse. Almost 150 countries – plus the European Union – have one. Their prominence has increased in the 1990s because of developments in central and eastern Europe. In other parts of the world, including southern Europe, military rule and dictatorships have variously given way to elected assemblies. 'Indeed, it may be that we are living in the "age of parliaments".'[2]

The increased prominence of legislatures has prompted a greater scholarly interest in their existence and what they do. There is a growing body of literature analysing the role of parliaments in the transition from one regime to another. There is some literature now on the role of national legislatures in the development of the European Union. There has also been some attempt to look at institutional change within established legislatures. Cross-national studies constitute a welcome advance in the study of legislatures. They help us to understand better the species of institution that is so pervasive. Yet such works constitute the poor relation within the field of legislative studies. They are dwarfed by the sheer body of writings on specific legislatures. We know a great deal about particular legislatures but very little about legislatures as legislatures. There is a mass of literature on the US Congress, analysing the institution from many perspectives, yet relatively little of that literature helps us generalise about legislatures. The literature that does help advance our understanding of legislatures as a particular species of institution is sometimes excellent but it is notable for its scarcity.[3]

Two principal conclusions flow from these brief introductory observations. The first is that legislatures are worthy of study. Their sheer number and historical persistence justifies some attention. The second is that such study has to be undertaken on a cross-national basis. That provides the basis for this study. The literature on legislatures also helps shape the focus and structure of the study. Though some parliaments are well studied, not least the British Parliament, the parliaments of western Europe have not been the subject of much cross-national study in recent years. An earlier volume, *Parliaments in Western Europe*, first published in 1990, has been reprinted.[4] A more recent work, *Parliaments and Majority Rule in Western Europe*, edited by Herbert Döring, provides a weighty compendium of data and testable propositions, informed especially by rational choice theory.[5] Beyond that, there is little literature that provides a straightforward description and analysis of the role of parliaments in western Europe.

The volumes in this series seek to advance our understanding of those parliaments. They do so by examining the relationship between parliaments and the other principal actors in a liberal democracy: governments, pressure groups and citizens. Governments are not particular to a liberal democracy but the relationship between parliaments and governments in such a system is qualitatively and quantitatively different to that in a non-democratic state. The first volume identifies and assesses the relationship between parliaments and governments, exploring especially the degree of specialisation within the legislature and its effect on the capacity of the legislature to scrutinise and influence government.

The second volume explores the relationship between parliaments and pressure groups. Pressure groups – or interest groups, to use a more neutral term – are intrinsic to a liberal democracy. Encouraging the creation and institutionalisation of such groups has been one of the core tasks of the new democracies in central and eastern Europe. Yet what is remarkable is the extent to which so little is known about the relationship between parliaments and pressure groups in western Europe. This may be because such activity is hidden, non-existent, or deemed to be of no importance, but it is important to know which it is in order to understand fully the workings of a political system.

The third volume explores the relationship between parliaments and the citizen. Though citizens may join pressure groups in order to give expression to particular interests and concerns, they have an independent existence as individuals in society. Though some studies have been published on the relationship between parliamentarians and their constituents in some European countries, they are usually chapter-length studies or articles. Few if any substantial works have appeared on the subject. Thus what may be considered one of the key relationships in a parliamentary democracy has gone largely unexplored.

Each volume thus adds to our understanding of the relationship between the legislature and a key body in a liberal democracy. In combination, they help identify the place of parliaments in the parliamentary democracies of western Europe. They help take us beyond a particular perception of legislatures as law makers and beyond specific country studies in order to appreciate the extent to which legislatures throughout western Europe serve as key components of the political web that holds together the democratic polity.

NOTES

1. See P. Norton (ed.), *Legislatures* (Oxford: Oxford University Press, 1990), p.1.
2. S.C. Patterson and G.W. Copeland, 'Parliaments in the Twenty-First Century', in G.W. Copeland and S.C. Patterson (eds.), *Parliaments in the Modern World* (Ann Arbor, MI: The University of Michigan Press, 1994), p.1.
3. On the literature that advances our understanding of legislatures, see Norton, *Legislatures*, and P. Norton (ed.), *Legislatures and Legislators* (Aldershot: Ashgate, 1998).
4. P. Norton (ed.), *Parliaments in Western Europe* (London: Frank Cass, 1990, pb edn. 1996).
5. H. Döring (ed.), *Parliaments and Majority Rule in Western Europe* (Frankfurt: Campus Verlag, New York: St Martin's Press, 1995).

CHAPTER 1

Introduction: Putting Pressure on Parliaments

PHILIP NORTON

Societies rarely comprise an undifferentiated mass of individuals. Individuals get together and form groups. The reasons why they do so differ. Some groups may be formed for mutual recreation and discussion. Some may be created to provide services to members. Some may be formed to help others. Some may be formed to promote a particular cause or idea.

Such groups may develop organisational characteristics: for example, meeting regularly, keeping records of proceedings, establishing leadership positions, hiring staff and developing means of keeping in touch with members. They may begin to take some action on behalf of their members.

The existence of such bodies is an intrinsic feature of a pluralist society. It is not surprising that the United States, where de Tocqueville noted the propensity of citizens to join groups and in which citizens are more likely than citizens of any other country to belong to groups,[1] is a breeding ground of pluralist theory. Groups are a distinctive and well established feature of Western society. In the new democracies of central and eastern Europe, where freedom of association was previously restricted or denied, establishing non-governmental groups or organisations has been central to the development of civil society.

Most groups are not formed for the purpose of influencing public policy. However, public policy impinges on groups in various ways – for example, their status for tax purposes, their capacity to conduct business – and groups may on occasion seek to influence the outcome of policy deliberations. Some groups may even be formed for the purpose of achieving a change in public policy. In west European states, groups attempting to affect the outcome of public policy are numerous. Groups will make representations to policy makers – an activity known as lobbying, after the place (the lobby just outside the legislative chamber) where influence-peddlers used to operate – to try to get them to accept their desired ends. Nor is such activity confined to the national level. State and local government are targets for lobbying by groups.[2] So too are the institutions of the European Union.

Group activity is thus an important part of the political environment of Western states. The institutions of the state are not politically autonomous. They exist in an increasingly crowded political environment, shaped and constrained by political parties and buffeted by demands for action from a myriad of organised groups.

Yet just how much are group demands directed at the central elected assembly – the legislature?[3] What is the relationship between parliaments and those groups attempting to influence public policy? The relationship is not one that has been the focus of much literature, either on parliaments or on policy analysis. It is this relationship that forms the basis of this study. Are parliaments ignored by groups or are they a magnet for group demands, and – if they are the subject of group demands – does that activity have any discernible consequence for the groups and for the parliaments? And what are the consequences of the relationship between pressure groups and parliaments for the political system?

PRESSURE GROUPS

The classic definition of a pressure, or interest, group is that it is a body that seeks to influence government in the allocation of resources without itself seeking to assume responsibility for government. This distinguishes pressure groups from political parties. Political parties do seek to assume responsibility for government and contest elections in pursuit of that goal.

INTRODUCTION

It is common to distinguish between sectional groups and cause groups.[4] Sectional groups exist to promote and defend the interests of a particular section of society, one usually defined by economic activity. Such groups are usually permanent, have a defined potential membership (all doctors in the case of a medical association, all lawyers in the case of a bar association) and frequently offer services to members (advice, information, discounted prices for goods and services, opportunities to meet and network with other members). Such groups do not have as their primary aim the influencing of public policy, but engage in such activity as and when it appears necessary to defend the interests of members. They have one important sanction they can deploy in their attempts to influence public policy: they can withdraw – or threaten to withdraw – their co-operation. A refusal by a group to co-operate in the implementation of a particular policy may make it difficult if not impossible for government to implement that policy. The clout of a particular group is maximised when its membership is close to the maximum potential membership.

Cause (or promotional) groups exist to promote a particular cause or idea. Where the cause is specific, the group may have a temporary existence: once the cause is achieved, there is no reason for the group to continue. Such groups are usually open to anyone who shares the goal of the group: thus the potential membership is the whole population. Such groups tend to lack the resources and the economic sanction of sectional interest groups: the threat to withdraw co-operation will not normally carry much political weight. They may, though, seek to have some impact by engaging in public demonstrations and, on occasion, civil disobedience.

The distinction is useful, though not watertight.[5] Some sectional groups are small and have little economic muscle. Some cause groups are large and permanent. There are groups that are difficult to categorise. Furthermore, with such a simple dichotomy, each category is remarkably broad.

A more sophisticated taxonomy has been offered by Wyn Grant. In a study of British pressure groups, he distinguishes groups in terms of their strategies for influencing public policy.[6] He draws a basic distinction between insider and outsider groups. Insider groups are regarded as legitimate by government and are consulted on a regular basis. Outsider groups are not consulted on a regular basis, either because they choose not to be involved in such consultation or because they are not regarded as legitimate by government.

In the first edition of his book, Grant refines each category. He identifies three types of insider group: high profile insiders (complementing government contact with the use of the mass media), low profile insiders (avoiding recourse to publicity) and prisoner groups (dependent on government or in the public sector). He also identifies three types of outsider group: potential insiders (wish to be insiders but have not yet won government acceptance), outsider groups by necessity (lacking the knowledge and skills necessary to achieve insider status) and ideological outsider groups (reject achieving change through the political process).

Grant's distinction between insider and outsider groups is not dissimilar to the distinction between sectional and cause groups, in that sectional groups tend to enjoy privileged access to government whereas cause groups have to resort to public pressure to get their case over to policy makers. However, the correlation between the status of sectional and cause groups and the relationship to government is not complete: not all sectional groups enjoy an established institutional relationship with government and not all cause groups are excluded from such a relationship. Furthermore, the distinction between sectional and cause groups is static. Grant's typology has the advantage of allowing for a change in status: a group may percolate from outsider to insider status or, indeed, be forced from insider to outsider status. Some groups previously treated with caution by policy makers may achieve insider status through public support or through demonstrating a sound command of the subject; some groups well regarded by government may lose their insider status as a result of a change of government or because of some change in the nature of the group.

GOVERNMENTS AND PRESSURE GROUPS

These typologies help give some shape to the many thousands of pressure groups that exist in Western countries. Grant's typology helps give some structure to the relationship of groups to

INTRODUCTION

government and, indeed, is premised on the existence of such relationships. The existence of potential insider groups implies that groups in that category accord some importance to achieving insider status. Groups want to have a close relationship with government. But what is there in such a relationship for government?

For pressure groups, access to government is necessary and possibly sufficient for achieving a change in public policy. Industrialisation, which occurred in Western countries at different times, generated a more specialised society. Interests became differentiated and organised. Sectional groups developed and began providing particular services to members. Many also began to take an interest in public policy. Manufacturers' associations, for example, were concerned about such things as taxation, tariffs and employment laws. Trade unions were interested in workers' rights. Such groups started making representations to government on behalf of their members. As such groups grew in number, the demands on government increased. The demands changed both qualitatively as well as quantitatively: not only were demands greater in number, they were also more specific and complex in content. Lobbying of government by pressure groups became – and remains – a notable feature of west European countries.

Groups need government if they are to achieve a change in public policy. Conversely, government needs groups. It needs groups for information, advice and co-operation. Governments rarely have the resources to compile data on activities in all the sectors covered by sectional groups. Groups may and often are able to supply that information. Government may also seek advice from groups, primarily sectional groups, on the feasibility of particular policies or on how certain problems may be addressed. Indeed, where a particular group has recruited to its maximum possible membership, it enjoys a virtual monopoly in terms of knowledge. 'If doctors are powerful', as Rudolf Klein noted, 'it is not just because of their characteristics as a pressure group but because of their functional monopoly of expertise.'[7]

Government is also frequently dependent on groups for co-operation in the implementation of policy. A refusal to co-operate may make it impossible to implement the policy effectively. However, such refusal is rare as problems are likely to have been resolved at an earlier stage through consultation. Insider status allows groups to make their views known directly, and usually privately, to policy makers and for policy makers to take those views into account in crafting a policy likely to prove acceptable.

Indeed, the relationship between groups and government is often symbiotic. Each needs the other. As groups have grown in number, governments in western Europe have tended to pursue the politics of accommodation, seeking to accommodate as many relevant interests as possible.[8] One consequence has been the co-option of groups into the policy process. In some cases, groups are given statutory representation on public bodies. In some countries, the representatives of organisations representing business and labour have been brought into a tripartite relationship with government. At a minimum, it is common practice – and, in some countries, formally required – for government to consult with affected groups prior to the introduction of a bill.[9]

The sheer scale of the exercise has also meant greater reliance is placed on the bureaucracy, as ministers do not have the time to devote to all the demands made of them by groups. More and more discussion has taken place in policy communities – comprising the representatives of the various groups in the sector and the officials from the relevant ministry – with proposals for change, usually some policy adjustment, being agreed and passed to the minister for approval.

Pressure for change does not always originate in groups. Governments may be committed to particular policies by virtue of popular demand or ideological belief. However, it is usually in their interest to solicit the support of affected groups. That support may be crucial in ensuring smooth implementation of the policy. It may also be valuable to government in selling the proposal to others in the political system. If a policy can be promoted as having the support of the relevant groups – the groups with the expertise in the field – it then becomes difficult, though by no means impossible, for others to challenge it.[10] Among those who may find it difficult to challenge the policy are members of parliament.

INTRODUCTION

PARLIAMENTS AND PRESSURE GROUPS

Industrialisation limited the role of parliaments in public policy making. It did so in two ways. It generated a middle class and a body of artisans who demanded a political voice. The widening of the franchise precipitated the development of mass-membership political parties. Parties acted as the conduit for the transfer of power from parliaments to party-dominated executives. The dominance of parties, with members being elected to parliament on the basis of a party label, sapped the political will of parliaments to challenge consistently and effectively the measures and actions of government. A parliamentary system of government is the norm in western Europe and a majority of members of a parliament are not willing to say 'no' on a regular basis to a government that is of the same political hue, or formed of parties representing a majority of the chamber. This development explains, in part, why government is the focus for group attention: government is the site of policy making. Once policy has been agreed and formulated by government, it is placed before the legislature for approval and that approval is usually forthcoming. The parliaments are not the site of policy making – in Mezey's terminology, they are reactive rather than active legislatures[11] – and party limits their capacity for substantial independent action.

Not only do parliaments normally lack the political will to challenge government measures, they also often lack the knowledge to do so. This brings us to the other consequence of industrialisation. Industrialisation, as we have noted already, produced a more specialised society. Interests became more organised and variously sought to influence public policy. The scale of the demands, and their complexity, were too much for a parliamentary assembly to cope with. A body of sometimes several hundred parliamentarians could not process and respond promptly to the growing body of specific demands. The greater the specificity and the complexity of the demands, the less easy it was for the member of parliament – usually not an expert in the subject – to comprehend the merits of the case. At the same time, the government was acquiring greater knowledge through contact with such groups.

7

What, then, of the present role of parliaments in relation to pressure groups? We proceed on the basis of two hypotheses. The first is that the developments we have described have pushed parliaments from the initiating and formulating stages of the policy process, leaving them operating instead primarily at the deliberative stage.[12] We have explored elsewhere the relationship between parliaments and governments.[13] As reactive legislatures, parliaments in western Europe respond to what government brings forward and the normal response is to give approval. There is some variation in the extent to which the parliaments constrain government – some exert greater influence than others – but the difference is relative. The more institutionalised parliaments have a greater capacity to constrain government than less institutionalised ones, but the constraint is occasional rather than regular and rarely if ever on matters of high politics. Although we have explored this hypothesis in depth in our other study, it does have a particular relevance for this volume. What flows from it is that government is the principal target for pressure group demands.

Our second hypothesis is that parliaments are a target for some group pressure because of their consequences for the political system. Although parliaments may now be limited in terms of policy making – what Robert Packenham has termed their decisional functions – they have other consequences for the political system; indeed, as Packenham has argued, these normally have greater significance for the political system than the decisional, or law-making, consequence.[14] We would expect a parliament to be attractive to pressure groups both as a target and as a channel. The distinctions are drawn from commercial marketing theory. A target is 'the person or institution who can bring about a desired change'. A channel is 'the person or institution who can influence them [the targets]'.[15] Parliament is a target in so far as it retains some independent capacity to affect outcomes. It is a channel in that it enables groups to attract the attention of the mass media and government.

Capacity to Affect Outcomes
Parliaments may be targets for lobbying because of their capacity to constrain government. Legislatures, by virtue of being legislatures, have the capacity to deny assent to measures of

public policy. The exercise of that power may be rare, but the fact that parliaments retain it may nonetheless make them targets – essentially of last resort – by groups that have failed to block a measure at an earlier stage.

If a parliament exercises its power to say 'no' to government, it is a blunt and negative weapon. Groups may seek to lobby parliaments to achieve a more positive outcome, either through an amendment to a government measure or the promotion of a private member's bill. Parliamentarians may be able to seek to change a measure, either through party mechanisms (parliamentary party group meetings) or through the formal parliamentary process (in committee or plenary session). Though rules vary, members – either a set minimum number or individually – may be able to initiate a bill. Groups may lobby members to introduce bills and may have bills ready drafted for the purpose.

Publicity

Members of a parliament may discuss at some length a particular proposal or a bill brought forward by an individual member or a parliamentary party group, even though the measure stands no realistic chance of being passed. The exercise can nonetheless serve some purpose. The debate is public and takes place in an authoritative forum – the nation's elected assembly. By virtue of parliament's status, the debate may attract the attention of the mass media. If the debate is heated and on a contentious issue – such as local taxation, immigration, abortion or homosexuality – it may prove especially attractive to journalists and the television cameras. Even though the issue may already be the subject of public debate and conflict, the legislature provides an important focal point for that debate and offers a legitimate focus for media attention. If the issue is not already the subject of public debate, then parliamentary attention may help get it on to the political agenda.

There is thus a value to groups in seeking to identify and mobilise supporters in the legislature. We would expect certain groups to be more likely than other groups to seek such legislative allies. Outsider groups might be expected to utilise this route more than insider groups. However, high-profile insider groups, by the very fact of being high profile, we would expect to seek a voice in parliament, whereas ideological outsider groups eschew such an approach. High-profile insider groups we would expect to be fairly sophisticated lobbyists, knowing which parliamentarians to approach, whereas outsider groups by necessity may lobby extensively but ineffectively, not knowing how or who to lobby in order to get their case raised in the chamber.

Interest Articulation
Members of parliament may also be useful means of articulating group views to government. Groups make representations directly to government. Depending on the standing of the group, those representations may or may not reach the appropriate minister. Groups may supplement that contact with indirect contact through members of parliament. Parliamentarians enjoy a formal status denied to officers of pressure groups. They may be able to elicit authoritative responses from ministers – for example, through questions or interpellations in the chamber, or by writing formally to ministers – in a way that pressure group representatives cannot. In the British House of Commons, for example, a letter from an MP to a minister has, by convention, to receive a reply from a minister. The letter has priority within the minister's department over other correspondence. Letters from those outside parliament may not even be seen by a minister, being replied to by civil servants in the minister's name.

Groups may also seek to utilise parliamentary committees, especially those empowered to take evidence. Groups may submit evidence to such committees and may even be called to present oral evidence. By speaking to such committees, groups may be hoping that parliamentarians take some action on their behalf – amending or initiating a bill, for example – but may also be attempting to reach government through getting their views on the record. Where committees are organised on the basis of policy sectors, usually paralleling government departments, we would expect a high level of activity by pressure groups.

The fact that west European political systems are parliamentary systems also has a relevance in this context. Ministers are typically, though not always, drawn from members of the legislature. In some, though not all cases, they remain within the legislature. Where they remain members of the legislature, they are likely to have to spend time in the parliamentary building. This physical proximity enables members to lobby ministers, not necessarily in the chamber but in the corridors and meeting rooms. If ministers attend meetings of parliamentary party groups, this may provide another opportunity for members to promote the views of particular pressure groups. Membership of the same institution and the status of membership will give members of the parliament some standing in requesting meetings with ministers, allowing them to encroach on ministers' time in a way that may be denied to those outside the parliament.

We thus have the basis for examining the relationship between parliaments and pressure groups in western Europe. The focus is not simply parliaments and pressure groups in western European nations but rather parliaments and groups in western Europe: that is, our coverage extends to the European Parliament, which is increasingly a target for pressure group activity. Our hypotheses – principally our second hypothesis – forms the basis for the first half of our study. Having seen to what extent our hypothesis is borne out by the evidence, we then explore the consequences of the relationship for parliament and the political system. Organised interests may be intrinsic and essential to a democratic polity, but are the consequences of their relationship to parliaments necessarily beneficial to the groups, to parliaments and to political systems?

CONSEQUENCES

We would expect the consequences of the relationship between parliaments and pressure groups to vary. There are perceived benefits for groups and parliament. If groups are rational, then their use of parliamentary lobbying delivers something of use to them. The benefits for groups are those that we have identified already: in pursuit of their goals, parliaments are targets and channels. MPs may be able to get a decision altered, they may help raise the public profile of the issue, and they can facilitate contact with ministers and their officials. The perceived benefits may extend beyond the purely rational to the symbolic or the egotistical: officers of groups may be attracted to the idea of spending time in the nation's parliament and of mixing with members of parliament, especially if the parliamentarians have a high public profile. Reports and photographs accompanying such activity may help officers to persuade members that they are active on their behalf.

For members of parliament, there are benefits in terms of information. Members of parliaments, both individually and collectively, have limited means to research information. No parliament in western Europe has the resources available to members of the US Congress. There is nothing on the scale of the Library of Congress nor a capacity – either on the part of committees or individual members – to employ research staff comparable to that enjoyed in the two chambers of Congress. In a number of west European parliaments, research staff are employed primarily by party groups and not by members individually.[16] Members may therefore be reliant on information researched by hard-pressed research assistants or by committee or library staff. The other main source of information is the government. Members of the governing party or parties may lack the political will to challenge government. Members of opposition parties may have the will but not the information that will allow them to do so effectively.

Pressure groups serve – or have the potential to serve – as a major source of information. The information they supply is normally self-serving, but then so too is that provided by government. Parliamentarians can assess for themselves the value of the information and choose between competing material: information from one group may challenge that provided by government or by other groups. A government may claim that a particular policy will have a certain effect: groups then lobby parliamentarians to argue that it will have a different effect. Without group activity, the parliamentarians would be less able to question government policy. The information supplied to parliamentarians may not only enable members to question government measures and policies but may also help to raise issues not on the government's agenda. The information itself may flow to members individually (for example, through a mass mailing or targeting) or to members collectively, in committee or parliamentary party groups.

For parliamentarians, there may also be a political and

psychological incentive to listen to pressure groups and pursue causes on their behalf. There may be a link, formal or (more likely) otherwise, between some groups and political parties. Pursuing the interests of those groups may bolster the standing of parliamentarians with those groups, and thus help the party. By pursuing particular issues, especially if they enjoy widespread public support – either nationally or in members' electoral regions or districts – members may help boost their image; even if it does not bring in extra votes it may prevent supporters from drifting away. It may also serve to make their reputation within the chamber. There may also simply be the satisfaction of having pursued a worthy cause.

There are also benefits for the political system. Allowing groups to engage in parliamentary lobbying may contribute to the stability of the system. Members of pressure groups are allowed access to the political system through parliament. They may also achieve access through bureaucrats and ministers, but not all groups have that access: as we have seen, outsider groups, by definition, do not enjoy that access. By making their case to members of parliament, pressure groups can at least get their voice heard. A letter from a member of parliament acknowledging the material sent by a group may in itself serve some purpose: a letter on official notepaper constitutes at least some link with the political process. More importantly, being permitted to give evidence to parliamentary committees links groups to the political process. It gives them a notable point of access and may absorb their energies in preparing material for the committees. If the evidence presented is then published or incorporated in the report of the committee, the more likely the group is to feel that the process is worthwhile. If parliamentarians table amendments to bills, or arrange meetings with ministers or bureaucrats on behalf of groups, the more likely those groups are to feel they have achieved something through their use of the parliamentary process. Even if the demands of the groups are not met, the fact that they have had an opportunity to make their case is important. Parliaments thus serve an important safety valve function, and that function contributes to the legitimacy of the system.[17]

However, we also anticipate that there may be problems in the relationship. For groups, making representations to members of the parliament may be an inefficient use of resources. Lobbying reactive legislatures, especially the weaker legislatures in the category,[18] may produce little in terms of policy outcomes or, for that matter, publicity or links with government. The perception of what the parliament can do may exceed the reality of what it can do. Even if on occasion lobbying parliament proves effective – resulting, for example, in a question being asked or a debate being initiated – it may nonetheless be inefficient. A group may expend substantial resources to achieve something that could have been achieved through the use of more sophisticated resources or knowledge. Those groups that are outsider groups by necessity are, we suspect, just as likely to lack the skills necessary to make the most effective use of parliament as they are to achieve access to government. Such groups may well lobby all members of parliament, for example, rather than identify those – sometimes very few – members who are likely to have an interest in their particular cause. Also, more significantly, fierce and unregulated lobbying may generate a negative public reaction, with – as we shall see – consequences for regime support.

There may also be problems for parliaments. Members may get partial information, either because of differences between groups or because of the activities of some of their own number. Strict pluralist theory assumes equality of access to the political system. In practice, access varies enormously. Some groups have resources that are superior (in terms of economic sanctions or their knowledge of the political system) to others. Some groups may not know how to achieve effective access (outsider groups by necessity), some do not want access (ideological outsider groups). Members of a parliament may thus receive information from some groups but not from others. In some cases, information may not be available simply because a particular body or interest is not organised at all. Where an interest is organised and has access to parliament, the information it supplies may be inaccurate or tainted. Groups may seek to put a particular gloss on the material (for example, by excluding embarrassing data) or may claim to speak for members without having sought the views of those members. In the United Kingdom, for example, the Automobile Association claims to speak for motorists but expresses its views usually without consulting its members.

INTRODUCTION

The material presented to members of parliament may also be tainted as a result of the activities of some of their own number. Some members may have close links with certain groups. Where several members have close links with the same group, this may give the group a disproportionately loud voice in parliamentary deliberations. Some members may also have professional or financial links with groups. Their advocacy on behalf of the groups may thus be self-serving and, in some cases, undeclared. By making use of their privileged position to advance the case for particular groups, members create an uneven parliamentary playing field for group representations. By doing so, and especially in cases where links with groups go undeclared, they may serve to undermine support for the parliament and the political system.

There is also another potential problem for parliaments: that of being overloaded with work. Material supplied by outside groups can be helpful to members, given that they have limited staff resources of their own. However, the very fact of having limited staff resources may mean that they have problems in sifting and assessing all the material that comes in. The more material that comes in, the greater the difficulty in sorting it. We would expect that once some groups start lobbying a parliament, others will follow (especially if the groups are promoting competing goals) and so the burden on the members of the parliament increases. We would expect the burden to be greatest for members holding key posts or serving on important committees, such as budget committees. Letters, telephone calls and visits from group activists take up time and there is an opportunity cost: parliamentarians have other tasks to be getting on with. Ultimately, the scale of the demands made by groups, and the volume of material they send, may prove too much for members of parliament to cope with.

There is also a danger in that group activity may undermine popular support for parliament and for the political system. If pressure groups appear to enjoy privileged access to parliament at the expense of individual citizens, or some groups enjoy privileged access at the expense of other groups, then we would anticipate that popular support for the institution will decline. That decline may be exacerbated if access is achieved through members of the elected assembly acting on behalf of groups because of financial links with those groups. Such links may be unethical but not illegal (in some cases, acting on behalf of a particular interest without declaring it), they may involve illegal activity (for example, bribery), or they may involve activity that falls in a grey area between the two: for example, what in the USA has been termed a 'deferred bribe', a company intimating to the member that a job will be available when he or she leaves the legislature. If such activity becomes public knowledge then public support for the institution is likely to be undermined, possibly – depending on the nature and scale of the activity – quite substantially, fuelling calls for reform or even fundamental change to the system.

What emerges from this evaluation is that parliaments need groups – without them they would suffer a severe information deficit – but they also need to ensure some degree of equity in access and treatment. Arguably, the challenge to parliaments is getting the balance right. Denying groups access to parliament causes severe tensions within the political system. Allowing them unregulated access has the same effect. Through the country studies in this volume, we can assess the extent to which parliaments have, or have not, achieved such a balance.

CHAPTER STRUCTURE

The chapters in this volume identify the nature and extent of the links that exist between parliaments and pressure groups. To what extent do those links support our two hypotheses? In particular, do groups make use of parliaments in the way posited by the second hypothesis? Do they supplement contacts with government with attempts to influence parliament; or is government the exclusive focus of their activity? And what are the consequences of the link between parliament and pressure groups? Are they in line with our expectations? Or are there consequences that we have not anticipated?

The chapters allow us to consider a number of west European countries in some detail. We have favoured depth over breadth. Comprehensive coverage would have required either study at a high level of generality or a volume largely unmanageable in terms of size. We have opted for a selected number of countries. This approach allows each author to present the results of a

INTRODUCTION

thorough examination, providing in some cases the first such study of the relationship between parliament and pressure groups. It also enables exceptions to our expectations to be identified and explained.

The range and number of countries are nonetheless such that they allow us to offer tentative conclusions. Given that we are selective in coverage, our conclusions cannot be definitive. But by covering the number of countries that we do, and in some depth, we can provide an overview and assessment of a neglected but important aspect of parliament's links with other actors in the political system. Our study thus has important heuristic value. It may also have a practical value. Through comparing the experience of various parliaments, we may be able to identify ways in which parliaments can achieve a publicly acceptable balance between closed and unregulated access for pressure groups. Pressure groups are essential to a democratic polity, but can the 'fit' between parliaments and pressure groups be better?

NOTES

1. G. Almond and S. Verba, *Civic Culture* (Boston, MA: Little, Brown, 1965), pp.266–306.
2. Indeed, the term lobbyist – though claimed by some to originate in Britain – entered American usage in the 1820s through favour seekers, dubbed 'lobby-agents', hovering in the lobby of the New York State Capitol at Albany; the term was shortened to 'lobbyists' and was soon in use in the US Capitol. Congressional Quarterly, *The Washington Lobby*, 5th edn. (Washington DC: Congressional Quarterly, 1987), p.2.
3. We use the term 'legislature' and 'parliament' as interchangeable throughout this volume.
4. J.D. Stewart, *British Pressure Groups* (Oxford: Oxford University Press, 1958).
5. See, for example, G.K. Wilson, *Interest Groups in the United States* (Oxford: Clarendon Press, 1981), pp.4–5.
6. W. Grant, *Pressure Groups, Politics and Democracy in Britain* (Hemel Hempstead: Philip Allan, 1989), pp.14–21.
7. R. Klein, 'Policy Making in the National Health Service', *Political Studies*, Vol.21, No.1 (1974), p.6.
8. J. Richardson, 'Convergent Policy Styles in Europe?', in J. Richardson (ed.), *Policy Styles in Western Europe* (London: George Allen & Unwin, 1982), p.202.
9. See Inter-Parliamentary Union, *Parliaments of the World* (London: Macmillan, 1976).
10. See R. Rose, *Understanding Big Government: The Programme Approach* (London: Sage, 1984), pp.83–1.
11. M. Mezey, *Comparative Legislatures* (Durham, NC: Duke University Press, 1979).
12. We assume a simple four-stage process of initiation, formulation, deliberation and

implementation. This derives from D.M. Olson, 'Parliaments and Policy: The Problem of Parliamentary Participation in the Policy Process', paper presented at the Conference on Parliaments, Policy and Regime Support, Duke University, USA, 1982. See P. Norton, 'Parliament and Policy in Britain: The House of Commons as a Policy Influencer', *Teaching Politics,* Vol.12, No.2 (1984), pp.205–6.

13. P. Norton (ed.), *Parliaments and Governments in Western Europe* (London and Portland, OR: Frank Cass, 1998).
14. R. Packenham, 'Legislatures and Political Development', in A. Kornberg and L.D. Musolf (eds.), *Legislatures in Developmental Perspective* (Durham, NC: Duke University Press, 1970), pp.521–37. We follow Packenham in defining functions in terms of consequences.
15. M. Lattimer, *The Campaigning Handbook* (London: Directory of Social Change, 1994). I am grateful to an excellent study by J.I. Elliott, 'Get the Message? Charities, Campaigning and the House of Commons', unpublished undergraduate dissertation, Hull University Politics Department, 1997, for this reference.
16. For a summary of the research and secretarial allowance available to members in various Western parliaments, including the USA, see Review Body on Senior Salaries, *Report No. 38: Review of Parliamentary Pay and Allowances,* Vol.2: Surveys and Studies, Cm 3330-II (London: HMSO, 1996), Table 2, pp.47–59.
17. See Packenham, 'Legislatures and Political Development'.
18. For a discussion of the ranking of legislatures within this category, see P. Norton, 'The Legislative Powers of Parliament', in C. Flinterman, A.W. Heringa and L. Waddington (eds.), *The Evolving Role of Parliaments in Europe* (Antwerp: Maklu, 1994), pp.15–32. See also Norton, *Parliaments and Governments in Western Europe.*

CHAPTER 2

The United Kingdom: Parliament Under Pressure

PHILIP NORTON

Pressure groups are well established features of the British polity. The Convention of Royal Burghs in Scotland, dating back to the fourteenth century, has been claimed as the oldest surviving pressure group in Britain.[1] The number of organised interests grew over the centuries – with cause groups, as well as sectional groups, coming into being – and became pronounced as a consequence of industrialisation.[2] Professional and employers' organisations were formed in the latter part of the nineteenth century. Trades unions, legalised in the 1870s, also organised and began to exert pressure on behalf of their members.[3]

As society became more specialised, so particular interests became more organised. By the early part of the twentieth century, interest groups were a notable feature of the British polity. Some – insider groups, in Grant's terminology – had developed links with government, while some cause groups, such as those demanding women's suffrage, had no such links. Insider groups were variously co-opted to the political process, sometimes being given a formal role by statute. For example, the Trade Board Acts of 1909 and 1928 provided for functional representation on such boards. The National Health Insurance Act of 1924 gave certain bodies, such as the medical profession, representation on committees appointed to administer the system of social insurance. By the late 1950s, more than 100 advisory bodies existed under statutory provision. The number swelled in the 1960s and 1970s. By the end of the 1970s, there were almost 2,000 advisory or executive bodies (the latter with power to make regulations or disperse funds) in existence,[4] representation on these bodies being determined by statute or by ministerial decision.

Such representation comprised only a part, but a formalised part, of the involvement of organised interests in the political system, with representatives of insider groups enjoying regular access to ministers and civil servants. Indeed, by the 1970s the extent to which such interests influenced public policy was a matter of public controversy. In 1976, Chancellor of the Exchequer Denis Healey sparked a political row when he made a three per cent reduction in the standard rate of income tax dependent on the acceptance of pay restraint by the trades unions. Critics accused him of giving power over taxation to bodies outside parliament.

Links between organised interests and government have become an established feature of the British polity. But what about the links with parliament? Organised interests have variously sought to influence parliament. In the eighteenth century, the interests were essentially economic ones, pressing for private legislation to authorise the enclosure of land. In the nineteenth century, public legislation began to dominate and various interests pressed government and MPs to introduce particular measures of public policy.[5] However, as political parties developed into mass membership parties and party began to dominate electoral and parliamentary politics, so groups came to accord priority to government as the target for their representations.

Members of parliament nonetheless continued to receive requests and demands from various organised interests. Many MPs, because of their own interests and backgrounds, had links with various organisations, such as religious, civic and professional bodies. The agricultural link was especially strong and also well organised.[6] So too were business interests.[7] The election of Labour MPs at the beginning of the twentieth century also gave a more organised voice to the interests of the trades unions.

Some organisations have appointed lobbyists to pursue their interests at Westminster. As early as 1910, the National Farmers' Union advertised for, and appointed, a 'Parliamentary Lobbyist'.[8] Whenever measures have been introduced affecting the interests of particular organisations, MPs have frequently received some representations from those interests. Some of these representations have been made in person by lobbyists. According to S.E. Finer, writing in 1958, 'Parliament swarms with the spokesmen of sectional interests – to a much greater extent, for instance, than the Congress of the United States'.[9] Such personal lobbying has been supplemented by letters and briefings from leaders or representatives of such groups or by mass lobbying by group members. The legislative process has been a particular target. In 1968, Stuart Walkland noted the extent to which the committee stage of bills was the occasion for the introduction of amendments on behalf of affected groups.[10]

Such activity was viewed as having some worth, otherwise a large number of organised interests were engaging in a purely worthless exercise. Making representations to MPs was seen as useful for making sure one's views were heard, especially when government appeared unresponsive. According to Finer, if government departments did not prove accommodating, then group attention turned to parliament, and if MPs did not prove responsive then groups appealed over their heads to their constituents. 'The public campaign – what the Americans call "grassroots lobbying" – is a comparative rarity in our country but it is on the increase.'[11]

However, there were other perceived benefits. Groups lobbied parliament to try to influence public policy on matters on which the government avoided taking a stance (for instance, some issues of public morality), on issues on which the government itself was divided and on issues on which government was still formulating a policy.[12] There was one notable occasion in the 1950s when lobbying of Conservative MPs persuaded a divided government to agree to the introduction of commercial television.[13] Several measures of social reform – the subject of lobbying, both for and against – were enacted in the 1960s through the medium of private members' bills, the government adopting, at least formally, a neutral stance.[14] Though such instances were rare, the prospect of some parliamentary action appeared to induce regular lobbying of MPs by organised interests.

Confining ourselves to the period from 1900 to 1970, we can draw three generalisations. First, that interests were frequently well organised. Second, that many organised interests recognised the value of seeking to influence public policy and that this was best done through government. And, third, that parliament was seen as a channel for representing views to government and, on occasion, a target for effecting outcomes on issues where government avoided taking a stance.

One other generalisation can be drawn. Although parliamentary lobbying delivered, or had the potential to deliver, some benefits to those doing the lobbying, the activity also aroused some public disquiet. There were two aspects to this concern: motivation and secrecy. For what purpose did MPs raise issues on behalf of particular interests? 'What induces Members to busy themselves at the behest of pressure groups? Is it certain that the motive is always altruistic? Venality can exist in any powerful assembly.'[15] Richards identified four means through which MPs could conceivably use their status for personal gain: by using government office to benefit business associates, pressing a minister to act in return for payment, by obtaining information not otherwise available for financial gain, and by pressing a minister to take action to the benefit of associates.[16] It was a breach of privilege of the House for any MP to accept money for the purpose of influencing any matter before the House but a great deal was left to the discretion of members. One MP described the relationship between MPs and business interests as the 'grey zone' and hoped it would not take a major scandal to require ministers to take a closer look at the problem.[17]

Allied to this was the fact that MPs were not required to disclose in all circumstances the links they had with particular groups. Not all MPs did so and it was recognised that in some circumstances (as with asking parliamentary questions) it would be too time-consuming if they had to do so. The extent of the anonymity embodied in the title of Finer's book, *Anonymous Empire*, nonetheless fuelled suspicion, leading Finer to call for 'Light! More light!'[18]

The relationship that existed between interest groups and parliament in the years up to 1970, and the popular suspicion that this relationship engendered, changed markedly in the years thereafter. The most dramatic change has been one of degree, but that has been such as to induce a change of kind. Since the 1970s, parliamentary lobbying has been a notable growth industry in

British politics and the scale and nature of it has fuelled demands, ultimately successful, for greater transparency in and regulation of links between MPs and outside interests.

PARLIAMENTARY LOBBYING

There are few objective data that allow us to demonstrate the growth in parliamentary lobbying. One indication is the growth in the number of professional lobbying firms, known as political consultancies. Though various organised interests had their own lobbyists, few firms of lobbyists existed before the 1970s. One of the earliest was Russell Greer, formed in 1970. 'Sadly, we were ahead of our time ... Russell Greer therefore struggled and the bank inevitably pressed.'[19] The growth period came after 1979. In 1980, what was to emerge as one of the biggest consultancies, GJW (formed by assistants to three former party leaders), came into being: by the mid-1990s it was employing more than 40 people. In 1982, one of the partners in Russell Greer, Ian Greer, a former Conservative Party constituency agent, formed his own consultancy, which soon established itself as one of the major lobbying firms: at its high point, in the first half of the 1990s, it had 50 employees and an annual income of £4 million. Another firm that was to establish itself as one of the leaders, Westminster Strategy, was formed in 1986 by six people who had left another consultancy: by the early 1990s, it too was employing more than 40 people. In 1987 it was estimated that the political consultancy industry was expanding by between 20 and 25 per cent a year.[20]

The creation of such firms raised the profile, and the visibility, of lobbying. In 1987, the leading annual reference book on Parliament, *Dod's Parliamentary Companion*, started listing 'Parliamentary Consultants'. In its first entry, it listed 13 firms. The following year, the number increased to 18 and the year after to 36. By 1994, the number was 45.[21] The increase in the number does not necessarily represent new firms coming into being (some had existed before but not been listed) but it is indicative of the greater visibility of such activity; and to some extent does reflect a growth in such firms. Some of the firms listed in the 1990s were public relations firms which had branched out into lobbying and some were newly created firms. Some of the firms were short lived;[22] most, though, continued to be listed in succeeding editions.

Most of these firms engaged in lobbying, or political monitoring, of government as well as parliament. However, one measure more pertinent for demonstrating the growth in parliamentary lobbying – indeed, something at the heart of such lobbying – is the increase in mail received by MPs from lobbying firms. Though there are hard data for the number of letters received by MPs, there is little data on whether the proportion from organised interests has changed over time. What evidence there is comes principally from long-serving MPs who have noted a massive increase in circulars and briefings from organised interests. In the 1950s and 1960s, incoming mail from such interests was not extensive. It grew in the 1970s and has continued to grow since. MPs elected in the 1950s and 1960s were not troubled much by such mail. One source suggested that in the 1950s an MP received fewer than 20 letters a week, principally from constituents.[23] That would suggest somewhere between 2,000 and 3,000 items of mail being received by MPs in one working day. By the early 1990s, the number of items of mail flowing into parliament each day was 40,000. Mail from organised interests (circulars, brochures, letters) constituted a large proportion, sometimes the largest proportion, of that mail. In 1986 one MP estimated, on the basis of the mail he received between August and October, that 'each MP receives a pile of unread lobbying mail per annum ten feet high'.[24]

The growth in lobbying of MPs was attested to by both lobbyists and MPs (the categories, as we shall see, are not mutually exclusive) interviewed by the Select Committee on Members' Interests in 1988 and 1989. In the view of two leading MPs, the change had been both quantitative and qualitative, with more lobbying taking place and in a form different to that of earlier years: lobbyists were more likely than before to write letters on behalf of organisations[25] and to organise meetings and receptions on behalf of clients in the Palace of Westminster.[26] The nature of such activity was variously attested to by lobbyists.

There is thus some evidence to suggest a significant growth in the lobbying of MPs by organised interests. There is much harder evidence to show the scale of that lobbying in recent decades. A survey carried out among more than 250 organised interests in 1986 found that three-quarters (189 out of 253) had 'regular or frequent contact with one or more Members of Parliament'.[27]

THE UNITED KINGDOM

Most of the firms undertook their own lobbying of MPs. Only one in five hired a public relations firm or consultant, and only one in eight hired a firm that dealt exclusively with parliamentary affairs. The activities of the political consultants thus appear to constitute a small part of an extensive lobbying exercise. A survey of 180 sizeable companies carried out in 1985 found that more than 40 per cent utilised the services of political consultants,[28] thus suggesting that the services of lobbying firms is, as might be expected, more extensive among commercial firms, given that they have the financial resources to employ them.[29]

The 1986 survey also revealed that organised interests had asked MPs to engage in various parliamentary activities on their behalf (Table 2.1). As can be seen from Table 2.1, more than 80 per cent of the organisations surveyed had asked MPs to table parliamentary questions and almost 80 per cent had asked MPs to arrange meetings at the House of Commons. Over half had also asked MPs to table amendments to bills and to table a motion. Approximately half had asked members to arrange meetings for them with ministers.

A survey of MPs in 1989 also tapped the influence of pressure groups. When questioned about why they tabled parliamentary questions, 47 per cent of MPs who responded said they 'often' or (more frequently) 'sometimes' tabled questions 'because they were asked to'. Just over two-thirds 'sometimes' tabled written questions because they were asked to and 15 per cent 'often' did so. Of those respondents who identified on whose behalf they tabled questions, half mentioned local interest groups and their constituencies, and 15 per cent identified national interest groups.[30]

Interest group involvement in parliamentary activity is not confined to a particular sphere or a particular procedure. Of groups questioned in the 1986 survey, almost half (49 per cent) of the groups that responded had presented oral evidence to a select committee; two-thirds (65.6 per cent) had submitted written evidence. More than 80 per cent of the groups said that there had been legislation in recent years that had been a cause of concern to them. Of these, two-thirds had sent circular material to all or a large number of MPs. More than half had asked an MP to table parliamentary questions about the bill,

TABLE 2.1
ORGANISED INTERESTS AND MPs:
REQUESTS TO TAKE ACTION

Request	Answering 'yes' [N = 189]	
	n	%
Question: Have you ever asked an MP to:		
Put down a parliamentary question?	157	83.1
Table a motion?	97	51.3
Introduce or sponsor a private member's bill?	70	37.0
Table an amendment to a bill?	117	61.9
Arrange a meeting for you or your organisation at the House of Commons?	148	78.3
Arrange a dinner or reception or similar function at the House of Commons?	78	41.3
Arrange a meeting with a minister?	94	49.7

Source: M. Rush (ed.), *Parliament and Pressure Politics* (Oxford: Clarendon Press, 1990), p.281.

speak in the second reading debate, and table amendments during committee or report stages. Almost half had arranged meetings or seminars with MPs.[31] More than three-quarters also contacted members of the House of Lords.

The extent of involvement of groups in lobbying during the legislative process has also been tapped by other empirical analyses and also by observation. A study of the passage of one particular bill – the Financial Services Bill in 1986 – revealed that more than 80 references were made by members of the standing committee to briefings and other representations they had received about the bill. One member estimated that the material received from outside bodies had been 'a couple of feet thick and may have amounted to a couple of hundred letters and documents'.[32] During committee stage, lobbyists could be seen regularly occupying seats in the public seating area and there was frequent contact between them and members of the committee, one MP being notable for the number of times he left the committee for consultations. Members of lobbying firms were also the principal occupants of the otherwise thinly attended public gallery during the report stage of the bill.[33]

Other case studies have also revealed sometimes extensive lobbying of MPs by outside groups, sometimes on a regular basis – as with the annual Finance Bill[34] – and on other occasions on particular bills. One of the most extensive and spectacularly effective lobbying campaigns took place to prevent passage of the 1986 Shops Bill to deregulate Sunday trading.[35] A number of organised interests, including churches and trades unions, combined to organise a campaign at constituency level, MPs being showered with letters from constituents and requests to attend meetings. When the bill came up for second reading in the House of Commons, 72 Conservative MPs voted in the opposition lobby and the bill was defeated – the first time in the twentieth century that a government with a clear overall majority had lost a second reading vote.

By the mid-1990s, lobbying of parliament was extensive and observably so. The extent to which the public seating in meetings of select and standing committees would be fully occupied could be predicted on the basis of the concern of the subject or bill under discussion to interest groups. A growing number of political consultancies occupied buildings within a few hundred yards of the Palace of Westminster. Mail continued to pour into both Houses. At least one MP found a normal wastebasket inadequate to contain the daily material from interest groups that was of no interest to him and used a plastic bin-liner instead. Letters and briefings were supplemented in some cases by mass lobbies of MPs, in some cases by vigils outside the Palace of Westminster when an issue was being debated. In February 1994, for example, after an extensive lobbying campaign by gay rights groups,[36] gay rights supporters held a highly visible candlelight vigil outside parliament while a reduction in the age of consent for male homosexual activity was debated.

We are thus able to make a plausible case that there has been an extensive increase in contact between interest groups and parliament over the past 20 to 30 years. We have fairly substantial evidence to show that the extent of lobbying of MPs by such groups is now extensive and is a marked feature of parliamentary life. Finer's claim in the 1950s that 'Parliament swarms with the spokesmen of sectional interests' was a gross exaggeration. In the 1990s, many MPs would not regard it as an exaggeration at all.

What, then, explains this remarkable increase in contact between interest groups and parliament? And what have been the consequences? Some of the consequences have been to the benefit of MPs, parliament and interest groups. However, there have been some distinctly negative consequences, most notably in the form of public perceptions of privileged access and conflicts of interest. Negative public perceptions have led to a much greater regulation both of MPs' activity and lobbying by organised interests.

EXPLANATIONS OF CHANGE

A number of developments external to parliament have resulted in interest groups turning their attention to parliament. Four in particular appear salient.[37] One has simply been a growth in the number of such groups. Of the groups listed in one directory of pressure groups published in 1979, over 40 per cent had come into being since 1960.[38] An increase in the number of groups would be expected to lead to an increase in the volume of lobbying in the political system, rather than an increase primarily in lobbying of parliament.

A second development has been a shift from distributive to redistributive policy. As the economic conditions of the nation worsened in the 1960s and the 1970s, so government pursued redistributive rather than distributive policies. Those bodies seeking a share of the increasingly limited resources thus had to compete with one another for those resources. That, again, might be expected to increase the volume of lobbying generally and, indeed, in so far as it was targeted, to increase lobbying of government, with parliamentary lobbying being supplementary to that activity.

The third development is possibly crucial in making parliamentarians more attractive to interest groups: the attempt by government after 1979 to achieve some degree of autonomy in policy making. A Conservative government was elected and sought to roll back the frontiers of the state and to move towards a market economy. To achieve its goals, it had to distance itself from organised interests. A number of organised interests, such as the trade unions, ceased to be consulted regularly by ministers and instead found themselves the target of government-inspired reforms. The perception that government was less amenable to group influence than its predecessors propelled groups towards parliament. If they could not achieve an input to policy deliberations through government departments, then they might be able to get their voice heard – and their views transmitted – through lobbying MPs. The House of Commons thus increased in significance as a channel for group influence.

And, fourth, there is the growth in the number of political consultancies. This growth may largely be seen as a consequence of the change in the nature of government, the firms coming into existence as a response to demand, though the existence of such firms may also have spurred more bodies to engage their services. The existence of lobbying firms emphasised the existence of lobbying and the firms themselves were busy selling the value of their activities to potential clients.

However, the explanations for the increase in parliamentary lobbying are not all external to parliament. There were developments within parliament that increased its attractiveness to interest groups. One was the increase since 1970 in independent voting behaviour by MPs.[39] The change was relative: MPs rarely voted against their own side, but the occasions on which they did so were more frequent after 1970. Occasions of cross-voting making a difference to the outcome were infrequent, but they were not unknown: even with the largest Conservative overall majority since 1935, the Thatcher government in 1986 could not prevent defeat on the Shops Bill. Knowledge that government backbenchers could induce some change, either by voting against the government or by threatening to, made them more attractive to groups lobbying for or against a particular provision.

Another development internal to the House, and especially relevant in the context of group input, was the creation of the departmental select committees in 1979.[40] For the first time, the House acquired a series of committees to examine all, or virtually all, government departments. Prior to 1979, groups wanting to get an issue raised in parliament had to try to locate sympathetic MPs and persuade them to employ some of the limited means available to them to raise issues. The new select committees offered a focus for group lobbying. Most select committees each had 11 members. There was thus a small body of MPs for groups operating in a particular sector to contact. Furthermore, select committees – unlike standing committees – could receive evidence. Groups could thus submit evidence during the course of a committee enquiry and may even be invited to present evidence orally. Once one group saw a competitor group present evidence, then it too wanted to submit evidence. As the assistant general secretary of the Trades Union Congress observed: 'Preparing and presenting evidence takes quite a lot of time, but it is difficult to ignore enquiries by select committees, not least because the TUC view needs to be expressed if other major organisations are expressing theirs.'[41] Evidence submitted to committees was normally published and thus on the public record. Also, select committees were empowered to decide their own agenda. Interest groups could thus make suggestions to committee members in the hope that a topic of concern to them might be selected for investigation.[42]

A third development has been the introduction of televised coverage of proceedings. Cameras were admitted to the House of Lords in 1985 and to the House of Commons in 1989. By raising an issue, an MP may attract the attention of the cameras. This is attractive to the MP, who wants to get noticed, and to groups wanting to get issues raised. If the group is based in the MP's constituency, then the greater the likelihood of the MP being willing to pursue the issue.[43] Groups issuing press releases about a particular issue may get little attention: if an MP questions the Prime Minister about the issue in the House, then the group may get extensive, and free, media coverage.

There is one other development that may have encouraged group interest in parliament, and it mirrors one of the developments external to parliament: the growth in political consultancies. Recent decades have seen a growth in the number of career politicians: those who live for politics and basically want to make a career in politics.[44] They seek election to parliament at an early age and stay until retirement. By the nature of their calling, they have usually few skills other than political skills. Given that MPs' pay has lagged behind managerial and professional salaries (until recently, an MP's salary was less than that of a headteacher of a sizeable school), and indeed had declined since 1964 relative to changes in average income,[45] MPs have variously sought to supplement their salary with outside earnings. For career politicians, this has meant offering their knowledge of parliament to outside bodies. They have thus accepted posts as parliamentary advisers or set themselves up as consultants. An analysis of the 1995 Register of MPs' Interests found that 26 MPs had consultancy agreements with public relations or lobbying firms and 142 had consultancies with other types of company or with trade associations. These 168 between them held a total of 356 consultancies. The 168 represented 30 per cent of backbenchers.[46] As with political consultancies, MPs may have taken up such positions as a response to requests from groups. Others, however, encouraged groups to take up their services, some MPs themselves being instrumental in forming political consultancies and touting for clients.[47]

The combination of these variables produced a remarkable increase in communication between organised interests and parliament. The change was significant and, as we shall see, had some remarkable consequences, but it also has to be seen in context. Lobbying of parliament was still, and is, viewed by groups as of secondary importance to lobbying directly ministers and civil servants. The 1986 survey of organised interests found that parliament was ranked fourth in order of importance in terms of seeking to influence public policy: the category of 'civil servants/government departments' came first in rank order, followed by 'ministers' and 'the media generally'.[48] The linkage between departments and interest groups remains strong and frequently institutionalised. Consultation papers and proposals for regulations are circulated usually to a large number of bodies. The concept of policy communities and the process of bureaucratic accommodation remain important to understanding policy making in Britain. Furthermore, in so far as interest groups lobby members of parliament, the MPs retain party as a protective shield against group pressures. In the event of a clash between party demands and group interests, the party will almost always come off best. However, parliament has in recent years become much more important to interest groups, partly as a target and, more especially, as a channel for getting views across to government and on occasion to the public. For groups, parliament is salient to their interests in a way that it was not 20 or 30 years ago.

CONSEQUENCES

What have been the consequences of this increased level of contact between MPs and interest groups? At one level, the consequences have been beneficial to parliament and to groups.

MPs have benefited, both collectively and individually, from the input of information from interest groups. By giving evidence to select committees, interest groups have ensured that the committees have information independent of ministers and civil servants. Interest groups have tended to provide the bulk of witnesses appearing before select committees.[49] Better informed committees and, through them, a better informed House of Commons are able to question government more effectively than would be the case if they had little or no independent information at their disposal. The same applies to material supplied by groups to members of a standing committee. Given the limited resources of backbench MPs, briefings by affected interests can ensure they are able to understand some of the implications of a bill in a way that otherwise they would not. Even where not fully conversant with a point being raised by a particular group, an MP may find it useful for tabling a probing amendment to elicit a government response on the issue. Even though not all information sent to a member will be relevant, the MP will retain that which is. Indeed, it is quite common for MPs, not least those serving on standing committees, to solicit information from affected groups.[50]

Groups have benefited from having an opportunity to get their views across and on occasion in getting ministers to respond positively to the case made on their behalf by MPs. If a reasonable case is made, ministers may accept a particular amendment to a bill or take on board a point with a view to introducing their own amendment later. At the close of proceedings on one bill, the minister conceded that the bill in many areas had been capable of improvement. 'When confronted with that argument', he said, 'I have tried to accept it with good grace.'[51] MPs have been able to elicit responses from government that groups on their own may not have managed and on occasion achieve substantive change. Of the organised interests surveyed in 1986, most – just over 55 per cent – rated their efforts in influencing legislation as either 'very successful' or (more likely) 'very successful'. Less than six per cent rated their efforts as 'unsuccessful'.[52] The links with select committees also elicited broadly positive responses, most groups believing that the impact made by their evidence to select committees had some impact: 16.3 per cent said it had a 'significant' impact and 69.2 per cent believed it had 'some' impact.[53]

This positive evaluation, coupled with groups according time and attention to committee activity (groups are especially avid consumers of select committee reports), ties groups more closely into the political process.[54] As such, parliament may be seen to be fulfilling a more important support function than before. By drawing groups more into parliamentary activity, it may also serve something of an educative function, groups not only learning more about parliament but also about other, sometimes competing, views than their own.[55]

However, the increased links between interest groups and parliament have also generated notable costs for the parliament. One has been in terms of resources. The other has been in terms of the popular legitimacy of the institution.

The demands made of MPs by interest groups has not been cost-free. Even at a very basic level, the time spent opening material sent by groups is considerable. Meeting with members of such groups also consumes MPs' time. One survey of 248 MPs in 1992 found that on average an MP spent over three-and-a-half hours a week meeting group representatives.[56] The requests made of MPs for information or to raise an issue, for example, through tabling a parliamentary question or an early day motion, adds to demands on the resources of the House and, in providing answers, on government departments. Some MPs in past years have hired researchers who also work as lobbyists, either as freelancers or as employees of political consultancies. These researchers then have had access to parliamentary resources, such as the library and parliamentary papers, that have been of some use to them in their lobbying capacity.[57]

The most severe negative consequence has been a decline in the popular standing of the House of Commons. We have already seen that some concern was expressed in earlier decades about the potential for abuse by MPs in using their positions to further the cause of outside groups. Such activity, with members benefiting financially from such activity, is not new,[58] but what caused increasing concern and public comment in the 1970s and

1980s was the nature and scale of the activity. Concerns about the role of MPs as advocates – especially paid advocates – of particular causes increased especially as the number of MPs hiring themselves out as advisers and consultants increased. In 1957, 18 MPs were known to be retained by public relations firms. By 1965, the number was at least 50.[59] Revelations about the links of a Labour MP with a firm lobbying on behalf of the Greek military junta in 1969 led to the creation of a Select Committee on Members' Interests. There was some greater openness as a result of the introduction of a Register of Members' Interests in 1974, brought in following another scandal (involving MPs and other public figures receiving payment from a corrupt businessman, John Poulson), but the extent of declaration required was limited and the revelation of links with organised interests served to heighten, rather than limit, popular concern.

The extent of public concern was variously tapped by opinion polls. A MORI poll in 1985 found that 46 per cent of respondents agreed with the statement that 'most MPs make a lot of money by using public office properly', against only 31 per cent who disagreed (23 per cent replied 'don't know'). Just over two-thirds of those questioned (67 per cent) agreed with the statement that 'most MPs care more about special interests than they care about people like you'. Less than one in five (19 per cent) disagreed with the statement.[60]

Stories about links between MPs and organised interests attracted critical press stories and a number of books, the titles reflecting the critical content: for example, *Corruption and Misconduct in Contemporary British Politics*,[61] *Westminster Babylon*[62] and *MPs for Hire*.[63] The links also attracted a growing body of academic literature.[64] Investigation of lobbying by the Select Committee on Members' Interests tapped unease about the activities of lobbyists among some MPs, some of whom gave voice to perceived misuse of Commons facilities by lobbyists.[65] Allegations of abuse were common, though rarely proven. In the 1986 survey of organised interests, almost 23 per cent of the groups involved said they were aware of abuses of the lobbying process in parliament, though the complaints focused primarily on privileged access through research assistants.[66] Only one respondent, relying on hearsay evidence, alleged any illegal activity. However, rumours of unethical behaviour – such as MPs accepting money to table parliamentary questions (the 'going rate' was said to be about £150 in 1985)[67] – were current throughout the 1980s and early 1990s.

There was some parliamentary response to the critical stories, primarily in the form of investigations by the Select Committee on Members' Interests. There were also a number of reforms implemented, notably in 1985 when MPs' secretaries and researchers were required to register details of outside paid interests. (By 1986, of 1,041 who had registered, 295 registered pecuniary interests.)[68] However, the register was not made public and few other substantive changes followed. The Select Committee on Members' Interests discussed the possibility of a register of professional lobbyists, eventually recommending in favour of such a register in 1991. Its recommendation was not pursued by the House and was overtaken by events.

In the summer of 1994, *The Sunday Times* ran a story revealing that a journalist posing as a businessman had offered 20 MPs £1,000 each to table a parliamentary question and two of them had not declined the offer. The story attracted extensive, and enduring, publicity. The two MPs were later suspended temporarily from the House. The controversy over what was dubbed the 'cash for questions' scandal was exacerbated when another newspaper alleged that two ministers had, when backbenchers, accepted cash to table questions and had not declared it in the Register of Members' Interests. One of the MPs admitted the claim and resigned his ministerial post; the other did not but was eventually forced to resign. The following year, a cabinet minister, Jonathan Aitken, resigned after being caught up in allegations over who paid for a visit he made to the Ritz hotel in Paris.

In October 1994, Prime Minister John Major announced the creation of a committee on standards in public life, comprising a number of distinguished public figures and chaired by a judge, Lord Nolan, to investigate and make recommendations as to any changes 'that might be required to ensure the highest standards of propriety in public life'. The committee reported in 1995[69] and its recommendations affecting parliament attracted opposition from a large number of Conservative MPs. (The recommendations affecting ministers proved less controversial and were accepted by government.) The report was the subject of two often ill-tempered debates in the House of Commons before the House voted to implement the recommendations (in one case going further than the committee recommended): a number of Conservative MPs joined with opposition MPs to ensure a majority for the proposals. The House voted to ban paid advocacy by MPs (MPs could still advise outside interests for payment but could not raise an issue on their behalf in parliament), to require disclosure of income derived from activities relating to their work as an MP (service as a parliamentary adviser had to be disclosed, within particular bands, but no disclosure of income was required from, say, being a farmer or an accountant), to establish a code of conduct, to create the post of Parliamentary Commissioner for Administration (to maintain the register, advise MPs and investigate complaints of breaches of the rules), and create a select committee on standards.[70] The new committee was formed as the select committee on standards and privileges, succeeding two previous committees.

The new committee was soon embroiled in investigating alleged breaches by some of the MPs caught up in earlier allegations, one in particular, Neil Hamilton, attracting headlines. The links between some of the MPs and one of the political consultancies, Ian Greer Associates, led to the collapse of what was, as we have seen, one of the biggest consultancies: Greer's company went into voluntary liquidation.[71] The investigation into Hamilton continued into the new parliament in 1997, even though Hamilton himself lost his seat in the general election. In the new 1997 parliament, one Labour MP was suspended briefly by the House after the committee on standards and privileges found that he had failed some years earlier to declare a business interest in the register.

The allegations of 'cash for questions' and the negative publicity surrounding MPs' links with outside bodies generated a negative public response. The committee on standards in public life noted that in a 1994 MORI poll the percentage of respondents agreeing that 'most MPs make a lot of money by using public office improperly' had increased significantly since 1985. In 1985, as we have seen, 46 per cent agreed with the statement. In 1994, 64 per cent agreed with it; only 22 per cent disagreed (Table 2.2).[72] The committee also drew on a 1994 Gallup

THE UNITED KINGDOM

TABLE 2.2
STANDARDS IN PUBLIC LIFE

Statement	% agreeing, disagreeing with each statement	
	1985	1994
Most MPs make a lot of money by using public office improperly		
Agree	46	64
Disagree	31	22
Don't know	23	14
Most MPs have a high personal moral code		
Agree	42	28
Disagree	35	59
Don't know	23	15
Most MPs will tell lies if they feel the truth will hurt them politically		
Agree	79	87
Disagree	12	8
Don't know	9	5
Most MPs care more about special interests than they care about people like you		
Agree	67	77
Disagree	19	12
Don't know	14	11

Source: Gallup polls, reproduced in *First Report of the Committee on Standards in Public Life,* Vol.1: Report, Cm 2850-I (London: HMSO, 1995), p.108.

poll which found that the overwhelming majority of those questioned believed it was wrong for MPs to take payment for asking questions in parliament (95 per cent deemed it 'not right'), to accept money or gifts in connection with parliamentary duties (89 per cent), or even accept payment for giving advice about parliamentary matters (85 per cent). The task of the committee was to try to restore public trust through recommending improved standards in public life. By accepting the recommendations of the committee, the House of Commons set in place mechanisms designed to restore public trust, even though not all MPs felt the changes were appropriate: some regretted the need to declare income, others objected to bringing in someone from outside to serve as a parliamentary commissioner. However, the recommendations were implemented and were fully in place by the end of 1996.

Changes were also brought in by the political consultancies. A number had for some time applied their own code of ethics (for example, refusing to hire an MP as adviser or consultant), but in response to increasing criticism of links between lobbyists and MPs they pressed for a compulsory code. When that was not forthcoming, they established in 1994 their own association – the association of professional political consultants (APPC) – and their own voluntary code. According to the association, its members account for around 75 per cent of fee income in the lobbying sector, which essentially means that most of the big consultancies are members. The association runs a complaints system with an independent disciplinary panel, and twice a year it submits a list of clients and advisers to the House of Commons and the Cabinet Office.

By 1997, a new regime was in place governing relations between MPs and organised interests. The changes were designed to create a wall between MPs and lobbyists, though MPs remained free to serve as advisers to outside organisations. The 1997 general election may also have served as something of a watershed. Most of the MPs that had been the subject of newspaper stories about their financial links with outside organisations retired or lost their seats (or, in the case of one member, was de-selected as a candidate by his local party). A new government was elected, proclaiming a commitment to probity and to open goverment.

CONCLUSION

Contact between pressure groups and parliament remains extensive. The return of a new Labour government in 1997, keen to move away from the association of the governing party with paid lobbyists, did not lead to any notable reduction in the activity of organisations lobbying for government action, nor in their contact with ministers and backbench members of parliament. As one lobbyist put it, ministers were keen to be seen to be consulting interests affected by government policy and backbenchers were keen to be seen to be active and, in the case of many new Labour backbenchers, just wanted something to do.[73] Some new MPs were especially keen to table parliamentary questions and motions for particular groups and causes, especially if they had a constituency base. The 1997 election also proved to be not quite the watershed that at first it appeared to be: within months of the election, allegations of misuse of parliamentary contacts by former Labour advisers turned lobbyists (including the leaking of drafts of select committee reports and offering access to key ministers) attracted extensive, and negative, media coverage.

Contact with parliament is still regarded as supplementary to contact with government departments – a channel rather than a target – but a useful point of contact nonetheless. Groups continue to lobby MPs to raise issues, to table questions, to introduce private members' bills, to put down early day motions and to arrange meetings with ministers. Select committees continue to make extensive use of witnesses from organised interests. In 1997, a Select Committee on Modernisation of the House of Commons recommended the more extensive use of special standing committees – committees that can take evidence – thus opening up the possibility for more formal input from outside groups during the passage of a bill.[74]

For many groups, contact is frequent and sometimes institutionalised. Some bodies, such as the Stock Exchange, lay on seminars or similar meetings for MPs. Both sides continue to benefit from the relationship. Groups find parliament a useful channel, and occasionally a target, and MPs obtain useful (as well as not so useful) information from groups. The relationship is now more substantial than before, better policed, and more transparent. Understanding of parliament, and its value to outside groups, remains imperfect, but arguably is now less imperfect than before.

NOTES

1. R.M. Punnett, *British Government and Politics* (London: Heinemann Educational Books, 1969), p.134.
2. G. Wootton, *Pressure Groups in Britain 1720–1970* (London: Allen Lane, 1975), Ch.2.
3. See Wootton, pp.75–98.

4. *Report on Non-Departmental Public Bodies*, Cmnd. 7797 (London: HMSO, 1980), p.5.
5. Wootton, pp.6–7.
6. See the extract from the 1910 Yearbook of the National Farmers' Union, in Wootton, pp.212–22.
7. See M. Hollingsworth, *MPs for Hire* (London: Bloomsbury, 1991), pp.3–4.
8. 1910 Yearbook, in Wootton, p.216.
9. S.E. Finer, *Anonymous Empire* (London: Pall Mall Press, 1958, 2nd edn. 1966), p.23.
10. S.A. Walkland, *The Legislative Process in Great Britain* (London: George Allen & Unwin, 1968), p.77.
11. Finer, *Anonymous Empire*, p.24.
12. P.G. Richards, *Honourable Members* (London: Faber, 1959), p.196.
13. H.H. Wilson, *Pressure Group: The Campaign for Commercial Television* (London: Secker & Warburg, 1961).
14. P.G. Richards *Parliament and Conscience* (London: George Allen & Unwin, 1970).
15. Richards, *Honourable Members*, p.196.
16. Richards, *Honourable Members*, pp.196–7.
17. Richards, *Honourable Members*, p.198.
18. Finer, p.145.
19. I. Greer, *One Man's Word* (London: André Deutsch, 1997), p.xiii.
20. *Parliamentary Lobbying: Third Report from the Select Committee on Members' Interests*, Session 1990–91, HC 586 (London: HMSO, 1991), p.ix.
21. In the two subsequent years, the number was less, the product apparently of moving from a simple listing to display advertisements.
22. There have been fairly substantial regroupings and mergers in the industry. See C. Grantham and C. Seymour-Ure, 'Political Consultants', in M. Rush (ed), *Parliament and Pressure Politics* (Oxford: Clarendon Press, 1990), pp.48–9.
23. Richards, *Honourable Members*.
24. Fred Silvester, Memorandum, *Parliamentary Lobbying: Select Committee on Members' Interests*, Minutes of Evidence and Appendices, Sessions 1987–88, 1988–89, HC 283, 518 (1987–88), 44 (1988–89), (London: HMSO, 1990), p.44.
25. See evidence of S. Orme, *Parliamentary Lobbying: Select Committee on Members' Interests*, Minutes of Evidence and Appendices, p.9. Sir R. Maxwell-Hyslop to author.
26. C. Onslow, *Parliamentary Lobbying: Select Committee on Members' Interests*, Minutes of Evidence and Appendices, p.1.
27. Survey Results, in Rush, *Parliament and Pressure Politics*, p.280.
28. *The Financial Times*, 23 Dec. 1985.
29. In some cases, where extensive monitoring and lobbying is required, firms may be paying political consultancies a six-figure sum.
30. M. Franklin and P. Norton, 'Questions and Members', in M. Franklin and P. Norton (eds.), *Parliamentary Questions* (Oxford: Clarendon Press, 1993), p.111.
31. Rush, *Parliament and Pressure Politics*, p.284.
32. P. Norton, 'Public Legislation', in Rush, *Parliament and Pressure Politics*, p.186.
33. Norton, 'Public Legislation', in Rush, pp.186–8.
34. See, for example, M. Rush, 'Influencing the 1986 Budget', in Rush, *Parliament and Pressure Politics*, pp.234–49.
35. See F. Bown, 'The Defeat of the Shops Bill, 1986', in Rush, *Parliament and Pressure Politics*, pp.213–33; and P. Regan, 'The 1986 Shops Bill', *Parliamentary Affairs*, Vol.41 (1988), pp.218–35.
36. The groups had been especially active in lobbying candidates during the 1992 election and in organising lobbying at constituency level. See M. Brown, 'The Age of Consent: The Parliamentary Campaign in the UK to Lower the Age of Consent for Homosexual Acts', *The Journal of Legislative Studies*, Vol.2, No.2 (1996), p.4.

THE UNITED KINGDOM

37. P. Norton, 'The Changing Face of Parliament: Lobbying and its Consequences', in P. Norton (ed.), *New Directions in British Politics?* (Aldershot: Edward Elgar, 1991), pp.65–6.
38. P. Shipley, *Directory of Pressure Groups and Representative Organisations*, 2nd edn. (London: Bowker, 1979).
39. P. Norton, *Dissension in the House of Commons 1945–74* (London: Macmillan, 1975); P. Norton, *Dissension in the House of Commons 1974–1979* (Oxford: Clarendon Press, 1980).
40. See G. Drewry (ed.), *The New Select Committees*, rev. edn. (Oxford: Clarendon Press, 1989).
41. D. Lea, 'A Trade Unionist's View', in D. Englefield (ed.), *Commons Select Committees: Catalysts for Progress?* (London: Longman, 1984), p.52.
42. See P. Norton, *Does Parliament Matter?* (Hemel Hempstead: Harvester Wheatsheaf, 1993), p.169.
43. We have already seen a constituency dimension to MPs' willingness to ask questions because they were asked to; there has also been a notable increase, in the period since proceedings were televised, in references to MPs' constituencies during prime minister's question time. M. Shephard, 'The Accountability of Ministers through Parliamentary Questions: Prime Minister's Question Time in the British House of Commons', Paper presented at the Second Workshop of Parliamentary Scholars and Parliamentarians, Wroxton, UK, 3–4 Aug. 1996.
44. A. King, 'The Rise of the Career Politician in Britain – And its Consequences', *British Journal of Political Science*, Vol.11 (1981), pp.249–85; P. Riddell, *Honest Opportunism* (London: Hamish Hamilton, 1993).
45. In 1995, average incomes were 80 per cent higher in real terms than in 1964, while the pay of MPs remained the same. Evidence of Sir T. Higgins, *First Report of the Committee on Standards in Public Life*, Cm 2850-I, Vol.1: Report (London: HMSO, 1995), p.22.
46. When a more long-standing arrangement – sponsorship of some Labour MPs by trade unions, usually involving payment of money to constituency parties – was taken into account, along with other payments to MPs for services rendered, it was found that almost 70 per cent of backbench MPs had financial relationships with outside bodies which directly relate to their membership of the House. *First Report of the Committee on Standards in Public Life*, p.22.
47. See, for example, the evidence of Sir M. Fox, *Parliamentary Lobbying: Select Committee on Members' Interests*, Minutes of Evidence and Appendices, p.197.
48. Rush, *Parliament and Pressure Politics*, p.294.
49. See Norton, 'The Changing Face of Parliament: Lobbying and its Consequences', p.73.
50. Norton, 'Public Legislation', p.197.
51. Norton, 'Public Legislation', p.191.
52. Rush, *Parliament and Pressure Politics*, p.285.
53. Rush, *Parliament and Pressure Politics*, p.283. See also I. Marsh, *Policy Making in a Three-Party System* (London: Methuen, 1986), pp.167–76.
54. Marsh, *Policy Making in a Three-Party System*, pp.169–71.
55. See Norton, 'Public Legislation', p.199. See also Marsh, *Policy Making in a Three-Party System*, pp.176–80.
56. P. Norris, 'The Puzzle of Constituency Service', *The Journal of Legislative Studies*, Vol. 3, No.2 (1997), pp.36–7.
57. See Grantham and Seymour-Ure, 'Political Consultants', p.77.
58. Hollingsworth, *MPs for Hire*, pp.2–8.
59. Hollingsworth, *MPs for Hire*, p.113.
60. *First Report of the Committee on Standards in Public Life*, p.108.

61. A. Doig, *Corruption and Misconduct in Contemporary British Politics* (Harmondsworth: Penguin, 1984).
62. A. Doig, *Westminster Babylon* (London: Allison and Busby, 1990).
63. Hollingsworth, *MPs for Hire*.
64. See especially Rush, *Parliament and Pressure Politics*, and G. Jordan (ed.), *The Commercial Lobbyists* (Aberdeen: Aberdeen University Press, 1991).
65. See *Parliamentary Lobbying: Select Committee on Members' Interests*, Sessions 1987–88, 1988–89, HC 283, 518 (1987–88), 44 (1988–89), (London: HMSO, 1990).
66. M. Rush, 'Parliament and Pressure Politics – An Overview', in Rush, *Parliament and Pressure Politics*, p.259.
67. Grantham and Seymour-Ure, 'Political Consultants', p.77.
68. *First Report from the Select Committee on Members' Interests*, Session 1986–87, HC 110 (London: HMSO, 1986), para.1.
69. *Committee on Standards in Public Life*, Vol.1.
70. *House of Commons Debates: Official Report (Hansard)*, Vol.263, cols.1723–39; Vol.265, cols.656–65. For a summary, see P. Norton, 'Parliament', in P. Catterall and V. Preston (eds.), *Contemporary Britain: An Annual Review 1996* (Aldershot: Dartmouth, 1997), pp.36–7.
71. See Greer, *One Man's Word*, and D. Leigh and E. Vulliamy, *Sleaze: The Corruption of Parliament* (London: Fourth Estate, 1997).
72. *Committee on Standards in Public Life*, Vol.1, p.108.
73. Lobbyist to author, 1997.
74. *The Legislative Process: First Report from the Select Committee on Modernisation of the House of Commons*, Session 1997–98, HC 190 (London: The Stationery Office, 1997), p.xiii. The committee also raised the possibility of some bills going to *ad hoc* select committees, which can also take evidence.

CHAPTER 3

Germany: Bundestag and Interest Groups in a 'Party Democracy'

THOMAS SAALFELD

Germany's political system has been described as a decentralised state in a centralised society: 'The dispersion of state power among competing institutions contrasts sharply with the concentration of private power in large social groups.'[1] Interest organisations are directly involved in the process of government, mainly through what Peter J. Katzenstein calls 'parapublic institutions'[2] such as the Federal Employment Office or the social welfare funds:

> Numerous institutions – corporate bodies, foundations, institutes – are organized under public law and carry out important policy functions. Chambers of Industry and Commerce as well as Agriculture, professional associations, public radio and television stations and various university bodies among many others express a general principle of organization: the independent governance by the representatives of social sectors at the behest of or under the general supervision of the state ... most of these efforts are part of an institutional design that seeks to link the responsibilities and jurisdiction of the state bureaucracy to well-organized social sectors.[3]

In many sectors, therefore, co-operation between government and socio-economic interests is relatively formalised. Consequently, some authors have argued that Germany fitted a 'neo-corporatist model' where public status is conferred upon

43

interest organisations and the agreements that they reach with government bodies.[4] While the policy consequences of this model are well-researched,[5] the implications for parliamentary democracy have long been a secondary concern of empirical research. In recent years, however, a number of empirical and theoretical studies have focused on the relationship between Bundestag and interest groups.[6]

This article addresses questions raised by Philip Norton in the introduction to this volume. Given the federal government's predominance and the important role of parapublic organisations in the policy-making process, is the Bundestag only a secondary target of interest-group activities? Is it a channel rather than the target of interest-group influence? Do interest groups supplement contacts with government with attempts to influence parliament; or is government the exclusive focus of their activities? To what extent are outsider groups barred from access to the parliamentary process? The evidence will be presented at three levels. In the first section, we shall look at formal and informal links between interest groups and the Bundestag as a whole. In the second section, the focus will be on links between interest groups and the parliamentary parties. The third level of analysis will be parliamentary committees. Throughout this article, the importance of political parties as a bracket between government and intermediary institutions will be emphasised. It will be argued that parties, inside and outside parliament, are important targets of interest group influence. The Bundestag's relationship with interest groups can only be understood properly if one considers the role of parliament's most important constituent parts – the parliamentary parties – in the process of interest aggregation and intermediation.

INTEREST GROUPS AND THE BUNDESTAG AS A WHOLE

There are three principal ways in which interest groups attempt to influence deliberations and decision making in the Bundestag: (a) they maintain close links with political parties; *inter alia* they try to ensure that a number of their officials are nominated as parliamentary candidates and, after their election, placed in the appropriate working groups of their parliamentary parties and, as a result, delegated to the relevant parliamentary committees ('internal lobby'); (b) formalised influence through, for example, participation in the Bundestag committee's hearings; and (c) influence through informal contacts with members of the Bundestag.[7]

Interest Organisations within Political Parties
All German parties have affinities to, and more or less formalised links with, interest groups. The Christian Democrats (the Christian Democratic Union – CDU) and its Bavarian 'sister party' (the Christian Social Union – CSU) and Social Democrats (SPD) maintain an extensive system of intra-party working groups which are organised around either certain policy areas or particular interests. The CDU, for example, maintains a number of 'associations' (Vereinigungen) such as the Christian-Democratic Employees (Christlich-Demokratische Arbeitnehmerschaft), representing workers and trade unionists; the Middle-Class Association (Mittelstandsvereinigung), mainly representing small business and the professions; the Economic Council (Wirtschaftsrat), representing the interests of big business and large employers; the Federal Committee for Agricultural Policy (Bundesfachausschuß für Agrarpolitik), representing agricultural interests; the Young Union (Junge Union), as the CDU and CSU's youth organisation, the Association of Christian-Democratic Students (Ring Christlich-Demokratischer Studenten) and the Pupils' Union (Schüler-Union), representing the interests of students and pupils respectively within the party; the Women's Association (Frauenvereinigung), promoting women's issues; the Senior Citizens' Union (Seniorenunion), articulating the interests of the elderly; the Working Group of Protestant Christian Democrats (Evangelischer Arbeitskreis), voicing the views of Protestant party members; the Association of Christian Democrats in Local Government (Kommunalpolitische Vereinigung) and the Association of Expellees and Refugees (Union der Vertriebenen und Flüchtlinge) as representatives of Germans who were expelled or had to flee from central and eastern Europe as a result of the Second World War. These intra-party associations have maintained close contacts with interest and pressure groups outside the parties. There has always been considerable overlap in leadership positions. Josef Schmid argues, however, that in recent years these interest groups within

the CDU have lost importance, while federal policy committees (Bundesfachausschüsse) have grown in importance. They are policy-specific clearing houses for competing interests within the party and prepare party policy in areas such as social policy, agricultural policy, youth policy or sports policy.[8] The organisation of interests within the CSU is very similar.

The Social Democrats have developed an analogous organisational structure. Like the Christian Democrats of CDU and CSU, they have used intra-party associations to integrate a number of, sometimes divergent, political and economic interests. Three associations are of particular importance: the Young Socialists (Jungsozialisten), representing the interests of younger party members under 35; the Association of Social Democratic Women (Arbeitsgemeinschaft sozialdemokratischer Frauen), representing the interests of women; and the Association of Employees' Affairs (Arbeitsgemeinschaft für Arbeitnehmerfragen). In addition, the party maintains an Association of Social Democrats in the Health Sector (Arbeitsgemeinschaft Sozialdemokraten im Gesundheitswesen); the Social Democratic Association for Local Government Affairs (Sozialdemokratische Gemeinschaft für Kommunalpolitik); the Association of Social Democratic Lawyers (Arbeitsgemeinschaft sozialdemokratischer Juristen); and an Association of Persecuted Social Democrats (Arbeitsgemeinschaft verfolgter Sozialdemokraten), representing the interests of party members who were persecuted under National Socialism and Stalinism.[9] Whereas the CDU and CSU's associations are predominantly bodies articulating socio-economic interests within the party, the SPD's associations have traditionally been more ideological.[10]

The organised representation of interests in the smaller parties is less formalised and specialised. Nevertheless, business interests are well represented in the liberal Free Democratic Party (FDP), whereas the Green Party (Bündnis '90/ Die Grünen) maintains close links to environmental pressure groups and groups campaigning on civil liberties issues.

Candidate Selection

Germany's electoral system is one of proportional representation with a two-tier districting system. Half of the 656 (1994) members of parliament are elected at the lower level by plurality vote (first-past-the-post system) in single-member constituencies. Proportionality of the outcome is achieved through adjustment at the upper level where the other half of deputies is elected from federal-state party lists. Since 1953 each voter has cast two ballots (1949: one ballot) – one for a constituency candidate and the other for a party.[11] The party vote at the upper level is used to calculate the percentage of parliamentary seats a party will receive. The mandates won in the lower-level constituency contests are then deducted from this total. Thus, parties winning a less than proportional share of seats at the lower level are compensated with a higher number of seats from the party lists at the higher level.

The representation of intra-party interests has traditionally been achieved through the placement of group representatives on the state lists. The composition of these lists cannot be controlled by the national or state party. The selection of candidates takes place at nomination conventions held six to eight weeks before election day. The delegates to these conventions are elected by the rank-and-file members. The state lists are usually the result of bargaining between the leaderships of the relevant district and constituency parties before these nomination conferences are convened. This process is heavily dominated by party elites. Especially in the Social Democratic Party (SPD), the Christian Democratic Union (CDU) and the Christian Social Union (CSU) attempts are made in these bargaining processes to ensure proportional representation for all-important intra-party interest groups as well as the major Christian confessions. More recently, there have also been attempts at SPD and Green nomination conferences to reduce the gender gap amongst candidates.

As a result of the nomination process and the fact that the representative of intra-party interest-group associations are often leading officials of a parallel interest group outside the party, the Bundestag has usually contained a large number of interest-group officials.[12] Table 3.1 lists the number of interest-group officials in the Bundestag between 1972 and 1994. On the whole, the data reveal a steady decline of the share of interest-group officials since the early 1970s. According to Wolfgang Ismayr's study of the Bundestag,[13] this decline has been accompanied by a proportional rise in the share of professional politicians, that is,

TABLE 3.1
INTEREST-GROUP OFFICIALS IN THE GERMAN BUNDESTAG (1972–94)

Type of interest group	1972–76 (%)	1976–80 (%)	1980–83 (%)	1983–87 (%)	1987–90 (%)	1991–94 (%)
Trade unions	16.4	16.0	16.6	11.9	2.9	2.4
Big business and employers	5.6	4.4	4.8	3.3	3.1	2.9
Small business	7.3	7.3	10.8	9.4	5.8	4.2
Professions	1.2	–	0.2	1.0	0.6	0.8

Note: 'Officials' are defined as persons who have full-time or voluntary functions at senior level: managing directors (*Geschäftsführer*) of interest groups, chairpersons of interest groups at national, federal-state or district level, members of executive boards. In addition, the category includes employees of interest groups, trade-union secretaries and representatives of intra-party interest associations. As a result of changes in the reporting requirements for members of the Bundestag, the method for calculating the shares of interest-group representatives for 1972–90 is not completely identical with the one used for 1991–94.

Sources: P. Schindler, *Datenhandbuch zur Geschichte des Deutschen Bundestages 1949 bis 1982*, 2nd edn. (Bonn: Presse- und Informationszentrum des Deutschen Bundestages, 1983), p.204; Schindler, *Datenhandbuch zur Geschichte des Deutschen Bundestages 1980 bis 1987* (Baden-Baden: Nomos, 1988), p.20; Schindler, *Datenhandbuch zur Geschichte des Deutschen Bundestages 1983 bis 1991* (Baden-Baden: Nomos, 1994), p.283.

members who, prior to their election to the Bundestag, had been employees of parties or parliamentary parties, political appointees in the civil service, employees in government think-tanks, former members of state parliaments or former members of state governments. Ismayr's tentative explanation for this negative correlation refers to the professionalisation of parliamentary politics: being a member of parliament has increasingly become a professional career with typical career stages. Interest-group representatives find it more and more difficult to secure high-ranking places on the parties' state lists without simultaneously running as constituency candidates, and without passing through the typical career stages of professional parliamentarians. Political parties serve as the major gatekeepers in a political career – much like professional associations. The parties' size, organisational structure, electoral success and internal norms determine an individual's chances to achieve political office. The path to parliamentary or ministerial office usually begins with extra-parliamentary party leadership positions at the local level and electoral office in local government. Political leadership positions at the local level are usually springboards to mid-level elite positions and eventually to a career either in the federal-state parliament (Landtag) or the Bundestag.[14]

Formal and Informal Contacts
Compared to the United Kingdom, interest-group activity in the German federal capital is relatively formalised. The total number of such groups is estimated to be around 3,500–4,000. Less than half of them are officially registered at the Bundestag (the 'lobby list') and therefore entitled to be consulted by the federal government and committees of the Bundestag. The number of accredited groups has increased from 635 in 1974 to 1,572 in 1994. The Bundestag is, however, not their primary target: their main addressees are the federal ministries, individual ministers, the media and 'allied' interest groups. The working groups and interest associations within the parliamentary government parties may also be an important target. The most important institutionalised form of influence on the policy process are the hearings routinely conducted by the federal ministries in the early stages of government legislation, when the government is legally required to consult relevant interests. Nevertheless, the Bundestag standing committees are allowed to conduct hearings of experts and interest-group representatives. These formal hearings will be dealt with in the third section.

The contacts between members of the Bundestag and interest groups are not entirely formalised, however. Members of the Bundestag have a large number of formal *and* informal contacts. Table 3.2 presents the results of a survey of 327 members of the Bundestag carried out by Dietrich Herzog and his collaborators in 1988/89.[15] Amongst other questions, members were asked what types of interest groups they had formal and informal contacts with. They were also asked to name specific interest groups if they wanted to or could. In Table 3.2, the responses are summarised in a number of categories. In total, members of the Bundestag mentioned 619 specific organisations. In 1,024 cases,

TABLE 3.2
CONTACTS BETWEEN MEMBERS OF THE BUNDESTAG AND
INTEREST ORGANISATIONS (1988/89)

Type of interest group	Specific group mentioned by respondents (n)	Category mentioned by respondents in general (n)	Share of groups mentioned specifically by respondents (%)
Employers	112	226	49.6
of which			
– industrial interest groups	74	158	46.8
– groups representing small business	38	68	55.9
Trade Unions	54	67	80.5
Occupational organisations	92	142	64.8
of which			
– agricultural groups	29	43	67.4
– other	63	99	63.6
Social, cultural, charitable and leisure groups	140	248	56.5
Religious communities	155	220	70.5
Citizens' initiatives	66	121	54.5
Total	619	1,024	60.4
Aggregated			
Sectional groups ('producer groups')	258	435	59.3
Promotional groups ('consumer groups')	361	589	61.3

Source: M. Hirner, 'Der Deutsche Bundestag im Netzwerk organisierter Interessen', in D. Herzog, H. Rebenstorf and B. Weßels (eds.), *Parlament und Gesellschaft: Eine Funktionsanalyse der repräsentativen Demokratie* (Opladen: Westdeutscher Verlag, 1993), p.150.

they referred to broader categories such as 'citizens' initiatives' or 'industrial interest groups'. Since multiple responses were possible, a certain degree of overlap is likely. On aggregate, members of the Bundestag had more contacts with promotional groups (361 specific and 589 general mentions) than sectional groups (258 specific and 361 general mentions). The categories most frequently mentioned were religious communities followed by social, cultural, charitable and leisure organisations. The sectional groups mentioned most frequently were groups representing industrial interests (74 specific and 158 general mentions). Trade unions, groups representing small businesses and agricultural organisations were mentioned least frequently.

GERMANY

It is interesting that industrial interests in general were mentioned 158 times, but only 74 members were able or willing to name specific groups. By contrast, members who reported contacts with trade unions referred to specific unions in eight out of ten cases (80.5 per cent), and members reporting contacts with religious communities named specific organisations in seven out of ten cases (70.5 per cent). These differences arguably reflect the greater fractionalisation of business and industrial interests, but also of social, cultural, charitable and leisure organisations and citizens' initiatives. In general, members of the Bundestag have contacts with a wide variety of different interest groups.

TABLE 3.3
FREQUENCY OF CONTACTS BETWEEN MEMBERS OF THE BUNDESTAG AND INTEREST ORGANISATIONS (1988/89)

Type of interest group	Average annual frequency of contacts per MP (n)	Frequency of contact with group in per cent of all contacts (%)	Frequency of contacts with group in per cent of sector (sectional/ promotional) (%)
Total	176.8		
Employers	41.2	23.3	42.4
of which			
– *industrial interest groups*	25.0	14.1	25.7
– *groups representing small business*	16.1	9.1	16.6
Trade Unions	32.6	18.4	33.6
Occupational organisations	23.3	13.2	24.0
of which			
– *agricultural groups*	8.5	4.8	8.8
– *other*	14.8	8.4	15.2
Sum of sectional groups	97.1 (54.9%)		100.0% = 97.1
Social, cultural, charitable and leisure groups	43.2	24.4	52.2
Religious communities	21.9	12.4	27.5
Citizens' initiatives	14.6	8.3	18.3
Sum of promotional groups	79.7 (45.1%)		100.0% = 79.7
N = 327	(100.0% = 176.8)		

Source: M Hirner, 'Der Deutsche Bundestag im Netzwerk organisierter Interessen', in D. Herzog, H. Rebenstorf and B. Weßels (eds.), *Parlament und Gesellschaft: Eine Funktionsanalyse der repräsentativen Demokratie* (Opladen: Westdeutscher Verlag, 1993), p.152.

Is this pattern of interest-group pluralism repeated, if we control for the intensity and frequency of contacts between MPs and interest groups? Table 3.3 provides data on the annual number of contacts the average member of the Bundestag had with a number of interest groups. On average, members of the Bundestag meet interest-group representatives almost 177 times (176.8) a year. Although the number of promotional groups they have contact with is higher than the number of sectional groups (Table 3.2), this relationship is reversed if contact frequency is taken into account (Table 3.3). Almost 55 per cent (on average 97.1, that is, 54.9 per cent) of their contacts are with representatives of sectional groups. The average member of the Bundestag meets representatives of employers' associations 41.2 times per year, which amounts nearly to one-quarter (23.3 per cent) of all contacts with interest groups. Contacts with trade union representatives account for almost one-fifth (18.4 per cent) of all contacts. Nevertheless, contacts with social, cultural, charitable and leisure associations remain the most important category (24.4 per cent). Yet, this category is a relatively broad one, comprising a large number of groups. On the whole, therefore, members of the Bundestag have more frequent contacts with producer groups, although the data suggest a relatively pluralist structure of contacts. The data certainly do not suggest a neo-corporatist pattern with privileged or indeed exclusive access of a few key sectional groups.

TABLE 3.4
MEMBERS OF THE BUNDESTAG AS NEO-CORPORATIST 'BROKERS' (1988/89)?

Individual contact intensities	No. of MPs	Per cent
No or infrequent contacts to key sectional interests	107	32.7
Exclusive contacts with trade unions	61	18.7
Exclusive contacts with employers	60	18.3
'Brokers'	99	30.3
	327	100.0

Source: M. Hirner, 'Der Deutsche Bundestag im Netzwerk organisierter Interessen', in D. Herzog, H. Rebenstorf and B. Weßels (eds.), *Parlament und Gesellschaft: Eine Funktionsanalyse der repräsentativen Demokratie* (Opladen: Westdeutscher Verlag, 1993), p.170.

To what extent is the German Bundestag characterised by neo-corporatist patterns of interest intermediation? Manfred Hirner attempted to 'measure' it by the extent to which individual members of the Bundestag have frequent contacts with both trade unions and employers' associations. He found that approximately one-third (32.7 per cent) of all members of the Bundestag have either no or only infrequent contacts with trade unions and employers' associations. An almost equal share of approximately one-fifth (18.7 and 18.3 per cent respectively) maintain exclusive contacts with either employers' associations or trade unions. Three out of ten (30.3 per cent), however, maintain regular contacts with both employers and trade unions. Hirner calls them 'brokers' whose activities are highly compatible with neo-corporatist patterns of interest intermediation. This conclusion is confirmed by his finding that there is a dominance of larger, established interest groups, although smaller groups are by no means excluded.[16]

Unfortunately, the empirical data available allows us to answer only the question: 'How important are interest groups to members of the Bundestag?' Representatives of interest groups were not interviewed. Therefore, there is no answer to the crucial question: 'How important is the Bundestag to interest groups? Is it a key addressee of interest group pressure, or just a supplementary channel which can be used if attempts at influencing government directly fail?' This is an area where further research is needed.

INTEREST GROUPS AND THE PARLIAMENTARY PARTIES

The two major parties in the Bundestag, the CDU/CSU and the SPD are considered to be 'catch-all parties' with a broad socio-economic base. They attract voters and members from all strata of German society. In practice, however, all parliamentary parties in the Bundestag – including the two 'catch-all' parties – have characteristic affiliations to particular interest groups. These party profiles could be summed up as follows: the Bavarian Christian Social Union (CSU) has particularly close links with agricultural groups, employers' associations, the two main churches (Roman-Catholic and Lutheran), as well as cultural and social associations. The Christian Democratic Union maintains particularly close links to employers' associations, the two main churches as well as cultural and social associations. The Social Democrats (SPD) are closely linked to the trade unions. The liberal Free Democratic Party (FDP) is characterised by close contacts with employers' associations, whereas the Green Party work closely with environmental and other citizens' initiatives.

TABLE 3.5
INTEREST-GROUP OFFICIALS IN THE PARLIAMENTARY PARTIES AND PARLIAMENTARY GROUPS* (1972–94)

Party	Bundestag term	Trade unions		Industry and Employers' Associations		Small business		Professions	
		N	%	N	%	N	%	N	%
CDU/CSU	1983–87	19	7.5	15	5.9	44	17.3	4	1.6
	1987–90	3	1.3	13	5.6	22	9.4	1	0.4
	1991–94	5	1.6	14	4.4	20	6.3	2	0.6
SPD	1983–87	43	21.3	0	–	1	0.5	1	0.5
	1987–90	11	5.7	2	1.0	2	1.0	0	–
	1991–94	10	4.2	1	0.4	2	0.8	1	0.4
FDP	1983–87	0	–	2	5.7	4	11.4	0	–
	1987–90	0	–	1	2.1	5	10.4	2	4.2
	1991–94	0	–	4	5.1	6	7.6	2	2.5
Green Party**	1983–87	0	–	0	–	0	–	0	–
	1987–90	1	2.3	0	–	1	2.3	0	–
	1991–94	0	–	0	–	0	–	0	–
PDS/LL	1991–94	1	5.9	0	–	0	–	0	–

Notes: 'Officials' are defined as persons who have full-time or voluntary functions at senior level: managing directors (*Geschäftsführer*) of interest groups, chairpersons of interest groups at national, federal-state or district level, members of executive boards. In addition, the category includes employees of interest groups, trade-union secretaries and representatives of intra-party interest associations.
* Because of its small size, the Party of Democratic Socialism (PDS/LL) was not recognised as a full parliamentary party. It had the status of a parliamentary group.
** 1983–90: Grüne; 1991–94 Bündnis '90/Grüne.

The latter's contacts to industry and small business are sparse, although there are some links to occupational groups and groups representing certain professions.[17]

Table 3.5 reports the number and share of interest-group *officials*[18] in each parliamentary party and in the 'parliamentary group' of the Party of Democratic Socialism (PDS/LL)[19] between 1983 and 1994. It reveals a marked decline of the share of trade union officials in both the CDU/CSU and the SPD. Although more than nine out of ten SPD members of the Bundestag are members of a trade union, the share of trade union officials fell from over one-fifth in the 1983–87 Bundestag to less than five per cent in 1991–94. In the parliamentary party of the CDU/CSU, the representation of trade union officials fell to almost insignificant levels, at least in quantitative terms. The SPD had only a small number of members with senior ranks in industrial, employers' or small-business associations. The CDU/CSU, by contrast, had a significant number of such officials on their benches. In the FDP, there was a relatively strong representation of small-business group officials.

These patterns are largely confirmed by the behavioural data presented in Table 3.6. There are a number of striking differences between the parties represented in the Bundestag in 1988/89: the total average number of contacts per year are highest in the CDU/CSU (205.1) and lowest in the FDP. Members of the CDU/CSU parliamentary party are particularly frequently in contact with employers' associations, professional associations, social, cultural, charitable and leisure associations and the main churches. Members of the SPD parliamentary party are most frequently in contact with trade unions and social, cultural, charitable and leisure organisations. The FDP has a clear tendency to focus its contacts on employers' associations, the Greens are in very close contact with citizens' initiatives.

In the CDU/CSU parliamentary party – the strongest parliamentary party throughout (West) German post-war history save the 1972–76 Bundestag – intra-party interest groups are highly organised along socio-economic lines. Intra-party groups in the SPD parliamentary party, by contrast, are also highly organised, but represent primarily ideological factions and currents. In the context of this study it is, therefore, particularly illuminating to refer to the internal organisation of the CDU/CSU

TABLE 3.6
CONTACTS BETWEEN MEMBERS OF PARLIAMENTARY PARTIES AND INTEREST ORGANISATIONS (1988/89)

Type of interest group	Average number of contacts per MP per year			
	CDU/CSU	FDP	SPD	Greens
Total	205.1	119.8	162.9	149.1
Employers	60.4	45.8	24.5	5.3
of which				
– *industrial interest groups*	33.8	27.0	18.4	4.4
– *groups representing small business*	26.7	18.8	6.1	0.9
Trade Unions	21.0	20.5	51.3	17.8
Occupational organisations	33.9	20.8	13.4	14.2
of which				
– *agricultural groups*	13.9	9.4	3.0	3.4
– *other*	20.0	11.4	10.4	10.8
Social, cultural, charitable and leisure groups	48.4	20.1	44.8	30.8
Religious communities	33.1	7.4	13.3	18.1
Citizens' initiatives	8.3	5.3	15.5	62.8
N	146	30	128	23

Source: M. Hirner, 'Der Deutsche Bundestag im Netzwerk organisierter Interessen', in D. Herzog, H. Rebenstorf and B. Weßels (eds.), *Parlament und Gesellschaft: Eine Funktionsanalyse der repräsentativen Demokratie* (Opladen: Westdeutscher Verlag, 1993), p.164.

parliamentary party.

There are five official intra-party interest groups within the CDU/CSU parliamentary party: the Employees' Group (Arbeitnehmergruppe), the Middle Class Discussion Circle (Diskussionskreis Mittelstand), the Group of Deputies Representing Expellees and Refugees (Gruppe der Vertriebenen- und Flüchtlingsabgeordneten), the Women's Group (Frauen-Gruppe) and the Working Group for Local Government Affairs (Arbeitsgemeinschaft Kommunalpolitik). All of these groups are linked to equivalent working groups of the party operating outside the Bundestag. The groups within the Bundestag elect their own officers, have paid staff (secretaries and research assistants) as well as funds from the parliamentary parties' budget. Like the chairpersons of the working groups within the parliamentary party (shadowing departmental standing committees and ministries), the chairpersons of the intra-party interest groups belong *ex officio* to the parliamentary party's executive committee.[20] In practice (though not according to the parliamentary party's rules of procedure), the chairpersons of the Employees' Group, of the Middle Class Discussion Circle and the Women's Group have a customary claim to one of the parliamentary party's deputy chairmanships. The Middle Class Discussion Circle is of particular importance and has considerable influence. In the 1983–87 Bundestag, for example, 23 out of 42 members of the parliamentary party's executive committee belonged to the Middle Class Discussion Circle, as did three out of seven deputy chairpersons of the parliamentary party, three out of four whips, 11 out of 17 chairpersons of the intra-party working groups. Moreover, in ten out of 17 working groups, at least half of the members belonged to the Middle Class Discussion Circle, and they had a majority in the working groups dealing with budgetary, financial and economic affairs. Although the economic interests represented in the Middle Class Discussion Circle are not homogeneous, it has considerable influence on the formulation of policy within the CDU/CSU parliamentary party. It monitors the government's legislative proposals in great detail and formulates its own position. It nominates rapporteurs (including some parliamentary secretaries of state) who promote the Circle's position within the parliamentary party and in the Bundestag's committees. It organises conferences and facilitates contacts with interest groups. In comparison, the influence of the Employees' Group is far less developed.[21]

INTEREST GROUPS AND PARLIAMENTARY COMMITTEES

The Bundestag mainly works through its specialised standing committees, which have a division of labour largely running parallel to that of the federal ministries. Only the Appropriations, European Affairs and Justice committees' terms of reference cut across departmental boundaries. Since 1969, the committees have had the capacity to include matters within their jurisdiction on the agenda that have not been specifically referred by the House as a whole (Selbstbefassungsrecht). This allows them to fulfil a watchdog function which is combined with the minute discussion of legislative drafts after first reading. About 60 per cent of bills are modified at committee stage.[22] Nevertheless, committees do not have autonomous decision-making powers.[23] They prepare recommendations for decision making on the floor of the House. The vast majority of legislative amendments made at the committee stage are related to details. More substantial amendments are usually initiated by the government or the Bundesrat.[24] Committees in the Bundestag do not initiate legislation, and the parties' positions are, in most cases, determined beforehand within their working groups and caucus meetings.[25] Nevertheless, committees provide the necessary infrastructure for communication and information between MPs, government ministers, bureaucrats and interest group representatives.

Committee Membership and Interest-Group Affiliation
The 'internal lobby' of members of the Bundestag who have been interest-group officials prior to their election, or who continue to be interest-group officials after their election, is most effective in the parliamentary parties' departmental working groups (see above, with regard to the CDU/CSU) and in the Bundestag's committees. There is a tendency in the parliamentary parties to nominate members, who represent certain interest groups, to serve on the 'appropriate' committees (Verbandsfärbung of committees). One author, therefore, has called those Bundestag committees that have a strong presence of related interests amongst its members 'interest-group islands' (Verbandsinseln).[26] Members with functions in, or close links to, employees' organisations such as trade unions have a disproportionately strong presence in the standing committees for Labour and Social Affairs, Youth, Family, Women and Health Affairs as well as in the Committee for Research and Technology. Officials of employers' and industrialists' organisations are over-represented in the committees for Economic Affairs and Finance. Along with representatives of small business, they have a strong presence in the committees for Appropriations, Transport and Research and Technology. The Standing Committee for Nutrition, Agriculture and Forestry is dominated by representatives of the Farmers Association, especially amongst members of the CDU/CSU. Empirical studies have found sufficient evidence to suggest that

interest groups find it useful to have their interests directly represented in parliamentary committees by members of the Bundestag.[27]

Nevertheless, it would be inaccurate to conclude that interest groups controlled the deliberative processes within parliamentary parties and committees. The effectiveness of 'internal lobbying' varies. Despite differences in emphasis, the two major parliamentary parties are characterised by a considerable internal pluralism of competing interest-group representatives. In particular, the interests of employers' associations, industry and small business are heterogeneous. Moreover, socio-economic interests are sometimes difficult to promote by MPs openly affiliated to a particular interest. Their affiliation is known, and they tend to be watched suspiciously by MPs representing competing interests. Social, cultural or charitable causes, by contrast, can be supported more effectively through 'internal lobbying' by sympathetic MPs – especially if the cause is promoted by MPs across the party spectrum.[28]

TABLE 3.7
PUBLIC HEARINGS IN THE GERMAN BUNDESTAG, 1949–90
(INCLUDING ENQUIRY COMMISSIONS)

	No. of public hearings	No. of different topics
1949–65	8	6
1965–69	58	28
1969–72	80	48
1972–76	76	51
1976–80	70	53
1980–83	51	41
1983–87	165	141
1987–90	235	185

Source: P. Schindler, *Datenhandbuch zur Geschichte des Deutschen Bundestages 1949 bis 1982*, 2nd edn. (Bonn: Presse- und Informationszentrum des Deutschen Bundestages, 1983), pp.604–6; Schindler, *Datenhandbuch zur Geschichte des Deutschen Bundestages 1980 bis 1987* (Baden-Baden: Nomos, 1988), p.483; Schindler, *Datenhandbuch zur Geschichte des Deutschen Bundestages 1983 bis 1991* (Baden-Baden: Nomos, 1994), p.716.

Hearings
The public hearings, which Bundestag committees regularly conduct, provide interest groups with formal access to the

chamber. Between 1949 and 1990, the Bundestag committees held a total of 654 meetings with public hearings. In these meetings, a total of 496 topics were dealt with. In addition, the Bundestag's enquiry commissions (Enquête-Kommissionen) held 90 meetings with public hearings.[29] Hearings are held in connection with approximately one-quarter of all bills.[30] Table 3.7 demonstrates that the Bundestag's standing committees and enquiry commissions have made increasing use of such hearings. Interest groups tend to use them as an opportunity publicly to present their position on a particular issue in a favourable light. Insider groups, in particular, do not have to rely on parliamentary hearings to promote their interests. For them, it is usually more effective to seek direct contact with the departments and the experts in the parliamentary majority parties.[31] For outsider groups, by contrast, public hearings may be an important arena to present their case.

Public hearings fulfil an important role as a source of parliamentary information, especially for the opposition parties. According to Paragraph 17(2) of the Bundestag's rules of procedure, a public hearing has to be held if it is requested by at least one-quarter of the committee members. This gives at least the major opposition party a chance to demand a hearing. The rules of procedure give each parliamentary party the right to nominate its own witnesses and experts, although the number of experts each party can nominate depends on its relative strength in the chamber. Thus, the majority parties are allowed to hear more witnesses and experts than the minority. Given the privileged access to government information enjoyed by members of the majority parties, public hearings are most frequently initiated by the opposition parties. Nevertheless, formal requests remain exceptional, hearings are usually scheduled as a result of negotiations between the parties' chief spokespersons in the committee. The publicity of hearings may reveal the intentions of interest groups which tend to influence government departments and the government parliamentary parties' working groups in private negotiations. Hearings may shed light on the negotiations taking place within the policy communities of experts in civil service, research institutions and interest groups. Evidence provided by its 'own' experts may allow the opposition to subject government policy to more effective scrutiny. The impact of hearings on policy depends on a number of variables such as timing and the government's commitment to a particular measure. New arguments and surprising changes are exceptional as all parties tend to nominate 'their' experts. The majority will therefore co-ordinate the questioning of witnesses and experts, and the opposition will have little chance to amend policy significantly. If the committee chooses to investigate an issue to which the government is not (yet) publicly committed, the arguments presented in a public hearing may well have a stronger impact on policy.[32]

CONCLUSIONS

The Bundestag is an important channel for interest groups seeking to influence public policy. It is not the primary target of interest group activity. Interest groups primarily seek to influence government and administrative bodies. In some policy areas, key interest groups are directly involved in policy implementation through their membership of para-public organisations. This is not to say that interest groups treat the chamber only as a medium to transmit their views in case direct access fails. A declining yet by no means insignificant share of members are interest-group officials and form what is often referred to as the Bundestag's 'internal lobby'. In the nomination process for Bundestag candidates, a number of interest groups make a considerable effort to ensure the placement of some of their representatives on the higher ranks of state lists. Above all, however, interest groups seek direct contact with political parties. The major parties of the Federal Republic, CDU, CSU and SPD, have an elaborate system of intra-party interest organisations giving interest groups access to policy formulation within the parties. The 'catch-all parties' especially are not simply transmission belts of socio-economic interests, but provide an arena for interest-group bargaining and serve to aggregate a multitude of interests which are often competing with each other. The SPD's attempt to modernise its programme and forge a compromise between its traditional trade union base and new social movements during the second half of the 1980s may serve as an example.[33] It is not difficult to find similar examples for the CDU.[34] In the major parties, organised intra-party interest associations are important channels and targets of interest-group activity. The CDU/CSU's formalised system of interest-based working groups within the parliamentary party is a unique case, although less formalised structures and processes can also be observed for the SPD. The smaller parties, Greens and FDP, are more selective in the nature and number of formal links with interest groups, but both parties are important targets for their respective clientele groups. For powerful insider groups, influence on the parliamentary parties, in particular, may enhance their capacity to affect outcomes in the policy-making process. This is the most convincing explanation for their attempt to be represented in the relevant working groups of the major parliamentary parties and, as a result, in the Bundestag's standing committees. Given the Bundestag's predominant self-definition as a 'working chamber' rather than a 'debating chamber', the publicity aspect of interest-group activity in parliament – the Bundestag as a forum of interest articulation – is less relevant than, for example, in the British House of Commons. Nevertheless, interest groups may use hearings to attract public attention for their cause, and outsider groups such as environmental groups have certainly managed to take advantage of the Green Party's presence in the Bundestag since 1983.

For members of the Bundestag, interest groups are valuable sources of information. In a 1988/89 survey, nine per cent of members said that publications by interest groups, trade unions and other organisations were amongst the three most important sources of information. The sessions of the Bundestag's standing committees and public hearings – to which interest groups are invited to give evidence – are amongst the important parliamentary sources of information.[35]

The data presented in the second section reveal that access to the Bundestag is not restricted to certain key groups. The contact activities of members are essentially compatible with a pluralist model, although each party has groups to which it has particular affinities. Martin Sebaldt aptly uses the term 'organised pluralism'.[36] The smaller parties, Greens and FDP, are slightly more selective in their contacts with interest groups.

Do members of the Bundestag feel interest groups have too much influence on the parliamentary decision-making process?

GERMANY

TABLE 3.8
INFLUENCE ON THE BUNDESTAG (1988/89)

Question: 'Nowadays, Parliament is exposed to a number of influences. Would you please tell us from your experience, which groups on this list have had too much or not enough influence on parliamentary decisions?'

	Influence too strong (number of responding MPs: 327)	
	No. of respondents mentioning item	Percentage (%) of respondents mentioning item
Civil service	208	64
Federal Constitutional Court	33	10
Parties	54	17
Trade unions	34	11
Industrial and business groups	90	28
Agricultural interest groups	140	44
Social movements and citizens' initiatives	9	3
Churches	19	6
Public opinion	48	15
Television	161	49
Press	126	39
Experts	20	6
Survey research	94	29

Source: D. Herzog, H. Rebenstorf, C. Werner and B. Weßels, *Abgeordnete und Bürger: Ergebnisse einer Befragung der Mitglieder des 11. Deutschen Bundestages und der Bevölkerung* (Opladen: Westdeutscher Verlag, 1990), p.120.

The data in Table 3.8 are taken from Herzog's survey of all members of the Bundestag in 1988/89. In general, members do not seem to be too concerned about interest-group influence. Approximately two-thirds think the civil service has too much influence; about one-half believe television's influence is too strong. More than two-fifths of all respondents consider agricultural interest groups to be too influential, whereas trade unions (11 per cent) and groups representing employers, industry and small business (28 per cent) do not rank amongst the top responses.

Unlike issues of party finance, the influence of interest groups in the Bundestag has so far not led to persistently adverse public reactions. Table 3.9 presents data from representative population surveys in which respondents were asked to state which

TABLE 3.9
PUBLIC PERCEPTIONS OF INTERESTS PURSUED BY MEMBERS OF THE BUNDESTAG (1982–91)

Question: 'Do you believe that the Members of Parliament in Bonn represent primarily the public interest, or do they have other interests which are more important to them?'

	Personal interest %	Public interest %	Party interests %	Other interests %	Don't know %
1982	22	40	2	10	26
1984	33	37	3	4	25
1987	34	32	4	7	27
1991 (West Germany)	24	43	3	11	19
1991 (East Germany)	24	35	5	12	26

Source: P. Schindler, *Datenhandbuch zur Geschichte des Deutschen Bundestages 1983 bis 1991* (Baden-Baden: Nomos, 1994), p.1362.

interests the MPs in Bonn primarily represent. Between 1982 and 1991, the modal category was usually the group who thought that the Bonn deputies represent the public interest. Not until 1987, in the aftermath of a number of scandals concerning donations to political parties, was the modal category the one stating that the members of the Bundestag primarily pursued their own personal interests. On the whole, between one-fifth and one-third of the population believed that the pursuit of personal interests were the deputies' priority. Compared to the categories 'public interest' and 'personal interest', the categories 'interests of MP's party' and 'other interests' (presumably including interest groups) remained relatively unimportant. This picture also seems to hold for east Germans after unification.

NOTES

1. P.J. Katzenstein, *Policy and Politics in West Germany: The Growth of a Semisovereign State* (Philadelphia: Temple University Press, 1987), p.15.
2. Katzenstein, p.58.
3. Katzenstein, p.58.
4. See, for example, Y. Mény, *Government and Politics in Western Europe: Britain, France, Italy, West Germany* (Oxford: Oxford University Press, 1990), pp.126–7. Mény uses Philippe C. Schmitter's definition of corporatism ('Still the Century of Corporatism?' *Review of Politics*, 36 (1974), p.93) 'as a system of interest

GERMANY

representation in which the constituent units are organized into a limited number of singular, compulsory, noncompetitive, hierarchically ordered and functionally differentiated categories, recognized or licensed (if not created) by the state and granted a deliberate representational monopoly within their respective categories'.
5. See, for example, Katzenstein.
6. See, for example, M. Sebaldt, *Organisierter Pluralismus: Kräftefeld, Selbstverständnis und politische Arbeit deutscher Interessengruppen* (Opladen: Westdeutscher Verlag, 1997); M. Hirner, 'Der Deutsche Bundestag im Netzwerk organisierter Interessen', in D. Herzog, H. Rebenstorf and B. Weßels (eds.), *Parlament und Gesellschaft: Eine Funktionsanalyse der repräsentativen Demokratie* (Opladen: Westdeutscher Verlag, 1993), pp.138–83; F. Müller-Rommel, 'Interessen gruppenvertretung im Deutschen Bundestag', in U. Thaysen, R.H. Davidson and R.G. Livingston (eds.), *US-Kongreß und Deutscher Bundestag: Bestandsaufnahmen im Vergleich* (Opladen: Westdeutscher Verlag, 1988), pp.300–323; B. Weßels, 'Kommunikationspotentiale zwischen Bundestag und Gesellschaft: Öffentliche Anhörungen, informelle Kontakte und innere Lobby in wirtschafts- und sozialpolitischen Parlamentsausschüssen', *Zeitschrift für Parlamentsfragen*, Vol.18, No.2 (1987), pp.285–311. On a more theoretical level, see Eberhard Schütt-Wetschky, *Interessenverbände und Staat* (Darmstadt: Wissenschaftliche Buchgesellschaft, 1997).
7. B. Weßels, 'Kommunikationspotentiale zwischen Bundestag und Gesellschaft: Öffentliche Anhörungen, informelle Kontakte und innere Lobby in wirtschafts- und sozialpolitischen Parlamentsausschüssen', *Zeitschrift für Parlamentsfragen*, Vol.18, No.2 (1987), pp.285–311; M. Hirner, 'Der Deutsche Bundestag im Netzwerk organisierter Interessen', in D. Herzog, H. Rebenstorf and B. Weßels (eds.), *Parlament und Gesellschaft: Eine Funktionsanalyse der repräsentativen Demokratie* (Opladen: Westdeutscher Verlag, 1993), p.142.
8. J. Schmid, *Die CDU: Organisationsstrukturen, Politiken und Funktionsweisen einer Partei im Föderalismus* (Opladen: Leske+Budrich, 1990), pp.260–67.
9. S. Heimann, 'Die Sozialdemokratische Partei Deutschlands', in R. Stöss (ed.), *Parteienhandbuch: Die Parteien der Bundesrepublik Deutschland 1945–1980* (Opladen: Westdeutscher Verlag, 1986), pp.2153–63.
10. T. Saalfeld, *Parteisoldaten und Rebellen: Eine Untersuchung zur Geschlossenheit der Fraktionen im Deutschen Bundestag (1949–1990)* (Opladen: Leske+Budrich, 1995), p.317 for further references.
11. Voters are able to 'split' their vote, that is, to vote for the list of one party and a candidate from another.
12. 'Officials' are defined as persons who have full-time or voluntary functions at senior level: managing directors (*Geschäftsführer*) of interest groups, chairpersons of interest groups at national, federal-state or district level, members of executive boards. In addition, the category includes employees of interest groups, trade union secretaries and representatives of intra-party interest associations.
13. W. Ismayr, *Der Deutsche Bundestag: Funktionen – Willensbildung – Reformansätze* (Opladen: Leske+Budrich, 1992), p.54.
14. Cf. D. Herzog, 'Der moderne Berufspolitiker: Karrierebedingungen und Funktion in westlichen Demokratien', in H.-G. Wehling (ed.), *Eliten in der Bundesrepublik Deutschland* (Stuttgart: Kohlhammer, 1990), p.34. Cf. also U. Hoffmann-Lange, *Eliten, Macht und Konflikt in der Bundesrepublik* (Opladen: Leske+Budrich, 1992), pp.402–3 *et passim*.
15. For general reference see D. Herzog *et al.*, *Abgeordnete und Bürger: Ergebnisse einer Befragung der Mitglieder des 11. Deutschen Bundestages und der Bevölkerung* (Opladen: Westdeutscher Verlag, 1990).

16. Hirner, pp.171–2.
17. Hirner, p.166.
18. For a definition of 'officials' see note 12.
19. A group of MPs is only recognised as a parliamentary party with full rights if its membership amounts to at least five per cent of the chamber. Because of its small size, the Party of Democratic Socialism (PDS/LL) was not recognised as a full parliamentary party in the 1991–94 Bundestag. It had the status of a 'parliamentary group'.
20. A brief description of the organisation of the CDU/CSU's parliamentary party can be found in T. Saalfeld, 'Bureaucratisation, Co-ordination and Competition: Parliamentary Party Groups in the German Bundestag', in K. Heidar and R. Koole (eds.), *Behind Closed Doors: Parliamentary Party Groups in European Democracies* (London: Routledge, 1998).
21. Ismayr, pp.104–9.
22. W. Steffani, 'Parteien (Fraktionen) und Ausschüsse im Deutschen Bundestag', in U. Thaysen, R.H. Davidson and R.G. Livingston (eds.), *US-Kongreß und Deutscher Bundestag: Bestandsaufnahmen im Vergleich* (Opladen: Westdeutscher Verlag, 1988), p.268.
23. The only committee with autonomous powers is the committee of selection, whose task is to select judges for the Federal Constitutional Court.
24. H. Schulze-Fielitz, *Theorie und Praxis parlamentarischer Gesetzgebung – besonders des 9. Deutschen Bundestages (1980–83)* (Berlin: Duncker & Humblot, 1988), pp.312–48.
25. N. Johnson, 'Committees in the West German Bundestag', in J.D. Lees and M. Shaw (eds.), *Committees in Legislatures: A Comparative Analysis* (Oxford: Martin Robertson, 1979), p.142.
26. R. Steinberg, 'Parlament und organisierte Interessen', in H.-P. Schneider and W. Zeh (eds.), *Parlamentsrecht und Parlamentspraxis in der Bundesrepublik Deutschland* (Berlin: de Gruyter, 1989), p.227; see also J. Weber, *Die Interessengruppen im politischen System der Bundesrepublik Deutschland* (Stuttgart: Kohlhammer, 1977).
27. Ismayr, pp.61–2; F. Müller-Rommel, 'Interessengruppenvertretung im Deutschen Bundestag', in Thaysen et al. (eds.), *US-Kongreß und Deutscher Bundestag*, especially pp.308–18.
28. M. Sebaldt, 'Interessengruppen und ihre bundespolitische Präsenz in Deutschland: Verbandsarbeit vor Ort', *Zeitschrift für Parlamentsfragen*, 1996, pp.658–96; W. Rudzio, *Das politische System der Bundesrepublik Deutschland* (Leske+Budrich, 1991), pp.59 and 78.
29. P. Schindler, *Datenhandbuch zur Geschichte des Deutschen Bundestages 1983 bis 1991* (Baden-Baden: Nomos, 1994), p.716.
30. Ismayr, p.480.
31. Ismayr, p.482.
32. Ismayr, p.480–81.
33. P. Lösche and F. Walter, *Die SPD: Klassenpartei – Volkspartei – Quotenpartei* (Darmstadt: Wissenschaftliche Buchgesellschaft, 1992), pp.125–31.
34. Schmid.
35. Herzog et al., *Abgeordnete und Bürger*, pp.76–7.
36. Sebaldt, *Organisierter Pluralismus*.

CHAPTER 4

Parliament and Pressure Groups in Italy

VINCENT DELLA SALA

The nature of the relationship between organised interests and the state has defied easy classification in post-war Italy. Conventional arguments suggest that Italy's 'weak' and poorly organised civil society in the immediate post-war years was easily penetrated and appropriated by the more structured political parties. The result was a form of pluralism that was largely an extension of the relations and dynamics of the party system. The space for autonomous interest groups was limited, especially for large producer groups such as trade unions. However, the argument continues, beginning in the late 1960s there began to emerge a degree of interest group organisation and activity that was relatively free of party intervention and control. Pressure groups found opportunities to influence policy in Italy's fragmented constitutional and political architecture. Forms of decision making began to appear that resembled corporatist structures, with the attendant access for insider groups. But decision making in a number of areas also was often fragmented, disjointed and open to a wide range of groups and interests; this reflected a weak executive in a constitutional and political landscape that had no readily identifiable epicentre. The fragmentation and diffusion of political authority created the conditions for parliament to be a focal point for interest group activity.

The aim of this chapter is two-fold. First, it will argue that the Italian Parliament is both a channel and a target of Italian interest group activity; and that despite significant political changes in the 1990s, there has not a been a drastic change in either of these

67

roles. Parliament retains some decisional functions, including in relation to budgetary matters. This has attracted the attention of insider and outsider groups looking to affect policy outcomes. Second, it will try to present some evidence of the ways in which the legislature deals with the demands emerging from organised interests. The chapter will demonstrate that parliament has a wide range of instruments that may be used to influence policy, ranging from simple written questions put to the government to drafting policy recommendations. As we shall see shortly, pressure groups would be ignoring a central site for influencing decision making if they chose not to focus some, if not all, of their lobbying efforts on parliament.

The discussion is divided into three main sections. The first will provide a very brief overview of the main types of pressure groups in Italy, and their relationship with the executive and parliament. The second part looks at parliament as a target and channel for pressure groups. The third section provides a brief sketch of the budgetary process to illustrate parliament's decisional functions and ways it may influence policy. The case study focuses on the incentives for pressure groups to choose the legislature as a site to pursue their interests.

PRESSURE GROUPS IN ITALY

Wyn Grant's typology of 'insider' and 'outsider' groups is particularly useful in trying to understand the relative position of various interests in Italy, their access to decision making and their relationship with the legislature.[1] Both sets of groups have found, in the highly permeable parliament, access routes to decision making. Moreover, the perceived or real threat of what Grant would call ideological outsider groups led to parliamentary reforms in the 1970s that helped increase the scope for parliament as a target of pressure groups in addition to enhancing its role as a channel.

The most obvious 'high profile insiders' in the post-war period, and certainly since the late 1960s, are the large producer groups such as trade unions and employers' associations. There was little consensus in the literature on where to place Italy on the pluralism–corporatism continuum.[2] Italy's consensual approach to decision making, especially in the period beginning in the early 1970s, seemed to provide special access to macro-economic decision making to 'insider' groups, such as the large trade union confederations closely allied to the three largest parties (CGIL with the Communist Party, CISL with the Christian Democrats and the UIL with Socialists).[3] Collective bargaining between labour and employers saw government play a decisive role in facilitating agreements between the producer groups through mechanisms such as social, fiscal and monetary policies. This was facilitated through a combination of mechanisms that included representative structures such as parliamentary committees; non-constitutional mechanisms such as tripartite negotiations; and non-institutional forms of political participation such as strikes and public protests.

It was the large producer groups that acted continuously to articulate demands on the government in key areas of economic and social policy. This continued into the 1990s as important tripartite agreements on pension reform, salaries and drastic cuts to public expenditures to meet the convergence criteria of the Maastricht Treaty led some to signal the return of 'concertation'.[4] For instance, it was trade union pressure that was partly responsible for forcing Communist Refoundation, a minor party whose support was crucial for government survival, to back down from its threat to defeat the centre-left government's 1998 budget in October 1997.

On the other hand, Italy's porous and permeable decision-making structures suggest that the centralised, coherent mechanisms that characterise most examples of corporatism do not apply. This refers not only to the diffusion of political authority to a number of different arenas but also to the nature of Italian capitalism. The presence of a large number of small and medium-sized firms, partly as a response to the increased social costs for capital emerging from tripartite agreements of the 1970s, meant that the employers were far from representing a homogeneous bloc.[5] In addition, the large state holdings in industry and finance created a group of state managers who represented a form of insider group whose interests may have been different from private sector employers. Tensions also began to emerge within the labour movement in the 1980s. This included a series of major defeats, such as the rebellion against labour leaders during the Fiat strike in 1980 and the defeat in a referendum on wage indexation in 1985; and the emergence of autonomous, and usually loosely organised, unions that took on the name COBAS (*Comitati di base*, or 'grass-roots committees') which did not fit well into the concertation mechanisms.

In addition to the high profile presence of insider pressure groups, there are a number of less prominent groups that have enjoyed privileged access to decision making. One of the best examples of this would be the group representing farmers, Coldiretti, who managed to have their members elected, mostly as DC parliamentarians. It was assumed that the Coldiretti would also play a role in choosing the Minister of Agriculture, along with the chair of the agriculture committees in the Senate and Chamber of Deputies. Similar low profile groups with strong links to the governing parties, but perhaps without the parliamentary presence of the Coldiretti, were those representing shopkeepers and small and medium-sized businesses. They represented an important base of electoral support for the DC, and its coalition allies; and this was translated into a degree of access in areas such as fiscal policy.

There is another kind of 'insider interest' that does not fit well into Grant's typology; that is, the entrepreneur as political actor. Two of Italy's richest men and heads of the country's largest private industrial holdings sit in parliament. Silvio Berlusconi's political career has been remarkable in that he managed, in a period that lasted less than six months, to start a political party (Forza Italia) and lead it to electoral victory in 1994. His stay in power as prime minister was short-lived, and he faced a constant stream of accusations of conflict of interests between his media empire and his political actions. Berlusconi continued to sit in the Chamber of Deputies as the head of the opposition in the 13th legislature (1996–). However, it is often overlooked that Gianni Agnelli of Fiat has been sitting in the Senate as an appointed lifetime senator since 1991. The presence in parliament of important industrial and financial figures is not isolated to these two cases, and it does raise the question of whether this is some form of 'insider' group. More problematic is whether this kind of privileged access to decision making constitutes some form of conflict of interest; especially as Italy has poorly formulated and implemented rules to handle possible instances where private and public interests may be in conflict.

An important development in the 1970s was that the relative 'weakness' of civil society that allowed the penetration by political parties in the 1950s and 1960s began to break down. A wide range of social movements and pressure groups looked to exploit the numerous access points made available to them by the fragmented institutional and constitutional architecture of the first Republic.[6] The result was what Grant might identify as 'outsider' groups increasing in confidence and access to decision making. The social unrest of the late 1960s caught not just the government and political parties but also trade unions unprepared to deal with the demands generated by an increasingly complex and fragmented society. Women's, environmental and students' movements were particularly good examples of interests that felt themselves to be marginalised by existing representational structures, and began to press their claims for a voice in decision making. What is important is that 'outsider' groups in Italy tended to be characterised as such not simply because of their relationship to the structures of decision making, but more so in terms of their links with political parties. For instance, the UDI (Italian Women's Union) had a long history of affiliation with the Communist Party, and this allowed it access to debates on issues such as child care and divorce. The period since the 1970s has seen a significant growth in the number of autonomous women's organisations that have often been in disagreement with the government and with the UDI. They were more ready to use all the instruments available to influence policy; and perhaps not as ready to accept consensual structures and processes.

The result of the proliferation of both insider and outsider groups is partly what David Hine has called, 'bargained pluralism'.[7] The inability of parties to aggregate demands as in conventional forms of party government, along with decision-making structures that were highly permeable to pressure groups, gave the impression of American-style pluralism. However, this was tempered by the privileged access of insider groups, and the ability of political parties to at least act as gatekeepers if not as vetoes at key positions such as in the government.

The brief discussion of the types of interest groups that have characterised the last three decades of decision making in Italy should help to shed some light on the relationship between parliament and pressure groups. The nature of Italy's 'insider' groups – many closely linked to particular parties and often engaged in direct contact with the executive – does not necessarily mean that parliament was bypassed as an important target and channel by pressure groups. As we shall see shortly, a fragmented political and constitutional architecture provided numerous access points to permeate decision making. It has been parliament, as the most visible representative institution and as an important gatekeeper in the policy process, that many groups have looked to in search of responses to their demands.

PARLIAMENT AND PRESSURE GROUPS

Parliament as Target
As Philip Norton has argued in the introduction, pressure groups will direct their attention to the legislature if they feel it will bring about a desired decision. Legislators will be targeted if they are seen to have the capacity to affect outcomes. As Norton also points out, the conventional view is that legislatures have lost some of their decisional capacity, thereby making them less of a target for pressure groups. The Italian Parliament may be a slight exception in western Europe.

We may begin the discussion of whether the Italian Parliament is a target by examining the extent to which it retains some capacity to affect decisions; put differently, is there some autonomy for parliament as a law-maker? One indicator may be found in the fate of private members' legislation relative to government bills. In most west European legislatures, the executive's legislative agenda dominates, and in many cases dictates, the parliamentary timetable. This is combined with party discipline to ensure that legislative decisions remain focused primarily on government legislation. This is not the case in Italy where government bills, with a few exceptions, are not afforded supremacy either by the constitution or by the parliamentary rules of procedure. Governments must negotiate with all the parties in parliament in setting the parliamentary calendar; this provides some room for negotiating time for the consideration of private members' legislation.[8] This feature of the parliamentary agenda is important in that it means that pressure groups may target private members, groups of members or opposition parties, in addition to the government, if they would like to put issues on to the legislative calendar. Moreover, they may look to opposition parties to use their role in setting the agenda to block proposed government bills even before they make it to the floor of the assembly or committee.

It is not only easier for private members' legislation to make it on to the parliamentary calendar, it also constitutes a significant portion of the legislation approved by the Chamber of Deputies in the post-war period. As the figures in Table 4.1 indicate, a little over one-third of bills approved in the chamber have been initiatives that have come from individual legislators and not government bills. Some caution needs to be exercised in assessing these figures. Private members' bills are often the result of compromises struck between parties, between the government and parties (or factions within parties), between the government and individual members. They do not mean that the government is completely marginal to this feature of law making. However, the figures in Table 4.1 do indicate that the executive does not have a monopoly on decisional functions. Pressure groups can, and do, use private members' legislation to meet their demands. For the most part, this has meant the production of what Giuseppe Di Palma has called microsectional legislation (*leggine*, or 'little laws' in Italy);[9] but it also has included important policy innovations such as maternity benefits for working mothers.

Moreover, neither the constitution nor parliamentary and constitutional convention have forced governments to resign in the face of defeats for their bills in parliament. Government defeats were made easier by the fact that until 1988 most votes were by secret ballot. Individual members could be lobbied by pressure groups to 'shoot down' (the term used for members of the government majority who used the cover of the secret ballot to vote against the government is 'sniper') proposals they wanted defeated; conversely, they could lobby opposition party members to vote in favour of proposals they wanted enacted. The secret ballot might also explain the high percentage of legislation that came from private members; legislators could defy their government's instructions to vote against private members' legislation without fear of sanction. The reform of the voting procedures has not meant that governments have had an

TABLE 4.1
GOVERNMENT AND PRIVATE MEMBERS' BILLS

Legislature	I 1948–53	II 1953–58	III 1958–63	IV 1963–68	V 1968–72	VI 1972–76	VII 1976–79	VIII 1979–83	IX 1983–87	X 1987–92	XI 1992–94	XII 1994–96
Private members' bills approved by Chamber	431	655	702	790	496	535	229	538	606	1,134	390	68
Govt. bills Approved (% of those presented)	1,996 (92.8)	1,439 (92.0)	1,340 (90.3)	1,259 (87.3)	663 (79.8)	94.1 (83.1)	644 (77.5)	861 (69.3)	769 (65.4)	922 (67.3)	292 (44.7)	318 (38.8)
Total approved private and govt.	2,427	2,094	2,042	2,049	1,159	1,476	873	1,399	1,375	2,056	682	386
% of total approved that are private members' bills	17.7	31.2	34.3	38.5	42.8	36.2	26.2	38.4	44.0	55.1	57.2	17.6

Source: Figures compiled by author from data found in Camera dei Deputati. Notiziario della Camera dei Deputati: Compendio Statistico dalla I alla XI Legislatura. Roma, 1994.

Camera dei Deputati. *Notiziario della Camera dei Deputati*. XII Legislatura. No.18 (March–May 1996).

easier time in getting their legislation approved. They continue to face obstacles presented by having few mechanisms, such as closure motions, to ensure that bills may be brought to vote. For instance, one tactic has been simply to stay away from the assembly, leading to a lack of a quorum for important votes, including those on the budget.[10]

Evidence of parliament's decisional functions comes from the use of decree legislation. In the period since the mid-1970s, Italian governments have resorted to the constitutional provision that allows them to issue decrees that have the force of law in cases deemed urgent or an emergency. The decrees expire after 60 days if they are not converted into ordinary law by both houses of parliament. In recent legislatures, about one-fifth of government bills approved in the chamber have been decrees converted into law.[11] More interesting for this discussion is the large number of decrees that expire without ever coming to a vote. As the figures in Table 4.2 indicate, this is the fate for most decrees; and more often than not they are reiterated as the government negotiates with forces in and out of parliament to mobilise support. Pressure groups, then, must not only focus their energies on the government that is issuing the decrees but also on parliament to ensure that legislators act on, or ignore, the government's provisions.

There is another feature of the Italian legislative process that attracts the attention of pressure groups; legislation may be approved in committee without having to return to the floor of the assembly.[12] Committees are less visible and their small number of members makes it easy for pressure groups to identify key members that they may try to target to achieve desired results. Committees have emerged as important gatekeepers of legislation, and they have drawn the attention of lobby groups. For instance, there is some evidence that shows that campaign contributions from sectional groups was often related to committee membership.[13] It also is significant that the large majority of private member bills approved by the Chamber of Deputies has been in committee, further reinforcing the claim that this feature of the legislative process promotes micro-sectional interests.

Italy's bargained pluralism has meant that all arenas where political interests and demands may find expression have been

TABLE 4.2
DECREES, 1948–96

Legislature	Decrees presented	Decrees converted	Decrees rejected	Decrees expired	Decrees reiterated	Reiterations as % of total
I (1948–53)	29	28	0	1	0	0
II (1953–58)	60	60	0	0	0	0
III (1958–63)	30	28	2	0	0	0
IV (1963–68)	94	89	2	3	1	1
V (1968–72)	69	66	0	3	4*	6
VI (1972–76)	124	108	0	16	5	4
VII (1976–79)	167	136	16	15	8	5
VIII (1979–83)	274	171	8	93	69	25
IX (1983–87)	302	136	30	99	92	30
X (1987–92)	459	187	15	249	207	44
XI (1992–94)	493	123	12	303	328	67
XII (1994–)	667**	121	9	511	n/a	n/a

Notes: * The total of the second to fourth columns may not equal that for the number of decrees presented as the do not take into account the fate of decrees that are carried over from one legislature to the next.
** May 1996.

Source: Figures compiled by author from data found in Camera dei Deputati. Notiziario della Camera dei Deputati: Compendio Statistico dalla I alla XI Legislatura. Roma, 1994.

Camera dei Deputati. *Notiziario della Camera dei Deputati.* XII Legislatura. No.18 (March–May 1996).

Camera dei Deputati. *La decretazione d'urgenza.* Roma, 1985.

sites targeted by organised interests looking to affect outcomes. For most of the post-war period, there was no political and constitutional epicentre that retained a monopoly on decisional functions. While the growth of the welfare state and the growing complexity of policy making favoured the executive, this did not translate easily into a strengthened executive.[14] It is not surprising that much of the discussion of institutional and constitutional reform since the early 1980s has centred on ways in which to place the executive at the heart of decision making; and to limit parliament's decisional functions. This has included changes to the electoral system, moving it in a majoritarian direction, and giving the executive greater control of the parliamentary timetable. However, change has been slow, allowing parliament to remain a central site in decision making and attracting the interest of pressure groups.

Parliament as Channel
While there has been a great deal of debate over proposals to limit parliament's law-making capacity, there has been little talk of curtailing procedures and mechanisms that may also serve to make it a channel for the interests of pressure groups. These include ways in which to publicise particular demands, as parliament is still the most visible institution for most citizens, as well as mechanisms for the articulation of interests.

Parliament's role as a tribune to put issues on to the national political and policy agenda is enhanced by a wide range of instruments available to carry this out. First, the relative ease for private members to introduce legislation and to get it debated in the legislature may fall within this category. In many cases, the aim in introducing legislation is not necessarily to effect an outcome, as this may seem unlikely; but it does serve to put the issue on the agenda. Moreover, for the individual member it is a way to respond to some pressure that has been put on him or her by an organised group. In many instances, the text of the legislation might even be prepared by the particular group for the legislator. The fact that the number of private members' bills presented to parliament continues to increase while the percentage that actually becomes law has been steadily decreasing suggests that presenting bills may be a way of channelling demands to the government and parliament.

There are a number of ways in which parliament may, as the central institution to debate the concerns facing the country, become the instrument used by pressure groups to create momentum for a policy change. The fact that the parliamentary timetable does not rest with the government means that there is an opportunity for pressure groups to try to get issues debated and receive national attention. For instance, Italian governments had, throughout most of the post-war period, avoided having any debate on family policy in parliament for fear that it would expose the great divisions that existed between the Catholic forces in the DC and the lay parties. It was a debate that the Communist Party (and later the Democratic Party of the Left) also wanted to avoid as it might upset the consensual basis for decision making in other areas. However, a broad range of pressure groups, from Catholic forces wanting to promote more traditional representations of the family to women's groups who wanted to press political actors to deal with the changing role of women in work and the family, continued to lobby for a national debate. The collapse of the DC made it easier for the pressure groups finally to get to the floor of the assembly an historic debate in 1995 on a series of motions presented by different groups of deputies.[15]

Lobbying parliament to publicise group interests took on a new perspective in the mid-1970s with the presence of the Radical Party as a small but vocal parliamentary group. The radicals defied easy description as a party. They had close links with a number of outsider groups that emerged from the social and political unrest of the late 1960s. The party, led by the charismatic and often erratic Marco Pannella, used parliamentary procedures along with extra-parliamentary forms of political participation and protest to draw attention to issues such as legalisation of narcotic drugs, civil rights, and famine in developing countries.

Pannella and the Radical Party contributed to exposing the fact that parliament may not be the only national forum that pressure groups could use to publicise their concerns. The Italian Constitution allows for an abrogative referendum to rescind any piece of legislation. Referendums are held after 500,000 signatures are collected, and the question and the signatures verified by the Constitutional Court. Referendums were used sparingly when they were introduced in the 1970s, but have grown exponentially in the 1990s. It is an effective way to put an issue on to the political and legislative agenda even if unsuccessful. More important for this discussion, it is a way for pressure groups to bypass parliament. A number of groups, such as environmental groups, have looked to the referendum as a way of getting around the legislature when it seems less predisposed to air 'green' concerns.

However, it is in articulating interests that parliament has the most complex relationship with interest groups. Here, the channel works in both directions as pressure groups provide an important source of information for the legislature and individual legislators that may be used in their relations with the executive. Legislators may also use various information-gathering mechanisms to transmit the concerns of pressure groups to the executive. While there has been a great deal of discussion about limiting the decisional functions of parliament, the tendency since the mid-1970s is to make greater and greater use of the instruments that may influence policy rather than affect decision making directly.

Table 4.3 presents figures representing the extent to which various information-gathering procedures have been used in parliament. The first set of data, which looks at written questions put to the government, reveals that legislators continue to present the executive with a large number of queries even though the likelihood of getting a response has been declining steadily. The written questions are one way to get the government's attention about a particular matter; they tend to deal with micro-sectional interests. It provides a resource that individual legislators may exploit to their advantage in relations with organised interests. They can claim they have transmitted a particular concern to the government through the question; quite often, this is all that is desired, which may explain why there continues to be a proliferation of questions without a response.

The second set of questions are those that require an oral response by the government in the assembly. These sessions are somewhat akin to Question Time in the British House of Commons. While they lack the dramatic tone of the British confrontational style, they do attract the attention of the national

TABLE 4.3
QUESTIONS IN PARLIAMENT

	I 1948–53	II 1953–58	III 1958–63	IV 1963–68	V 1968–72	VI 1972–76	VII 1976–79	VIII 1979–83	IX 1983–87	X 1987–92	XI 1992–94	XII 1994–96
Written questions in parliament	12,472	33,314	28,662	27,125	22,078	17,253	7,736	20,204	21,812	31,750	21,619	19,106
Responded	12,088	24,125	24,195	20,759	15,005	10,461	4,380	10,673	11,725	14,399	4,982	5,077
% responded	96.9	86.4	84.4	76.5	68.0	60.6	56.6	52.8	53.8	45.3	23.0	25.9
Oral questions	5,468	4,198	5,427	7,318	5,814	4,608	3,831	7,886	3,473	3,547	1,646	871
Responded	2,404	1,433	1,870	2,094	977	788	1,467	1,819	1,020	990	407	212
% responded	44.0	34.1	34.5	28.6	16.8	17.1	38.3	23.1	29.4	28.0	24.7	24.3

Source: Figures compiled by author from data found in Camera dei Deputati. Notiziario della Camera dei Deputati: Compendio Statistico dalla I alla XI Legislatura. Roma, 1994.

Camera dei Deputati. Notiziario della Camera dei Deputati. XII. legislatura. No. 18 (March–May 1996).

media. They are, then, a good way for pressure groups to lobby individual legislators to put government policy under close scrutiny. There has been no scandal such as the one in Britain of parliamentarians being paid to ask questions on behalf of organised interests (see Chapter 2), partly because there is a recognition that particular members represent specific interests such as the agricultural sector. The fact that members of Forza Italia can ask the government questions about its broadcasting policy when their leader heads the largest private broadcasting group in the country is an indication that oral questions in parliament can be used to channel demands directly on to the national political scene. Moreover, it also indicates a greater ambivalence about the use of insider status to promote private, sectoral interests.

The parliamentary committee system also provides ample opportunities for links to be established between pressure groups, the executive and legislators.[16] While these are nowhere near the 'iron triangles' that are said to characterise the US Congress, some committees have evolved into important gateways for policy. This is especially the case for the Budget Committee of the Chamber of Deputies, which has developed a number of practices that have made it an important channel for government policy to be transmitted to important social and political actors; and vice versa. For instance, the biannual appearance of the governor of the Bank of Italy to discuss monetary policy has become a major event that draws the attention not just of the national media but also trade unions and employers' associations. These groups lobby committee members to press the governor on particular issues; and the governor uses the appearance before the committee to inform groups of the direction that monetary policy is likely to take in the near future.

Another important mechanism for influencing policy through parliament has been the bicameral committees that have dealt with a range of topics from regional policy to organised crime. The bicameral committees not only scrutinise government activity; in some instances, such as the Radio and Television Broadcasting Committee, they are charged with drawing up specific policy recommendations for the government. The links developed with organised interests and government departments in this area of policy work make the parliamentary committees an important meeting point for most, if not all, the key interests in a specific policy area.

Between the First and Second Republics
The breadth and scope of changes to the Italian political, institutional and party systems in the 1990s have led to the conventional view that Italy's post-war constitutional order has come to an end even though a new constitution is not yet in place. This does not mean that there is a constitutional vacuum, but that there remains a certain degree of uncertainty in the transition to what is referred to as the 'second' Republic. A bicameral committee studying constitutional change agreed in principle in the first half of 1997 to changes that will make Italy a federal republic with a form of semi-presidentalism similar to that in France. In addition to the institutional changes being considered, there has been a radical transformation of the parliamentary class in the 1990s, with all of the major parties disappearing or changing name; and a significant turnover of deputies and senators.[17]

However, despite these changes in parties and personnel, parliamentary activity and behaviour, as seen in the tables presented above, has remained fairly consistent in most cases. More specifically, the main instruments for pressure groups to target parliament and to use it as a channel for their demands have remained very much in place. As the evidence presented in the various tables listed above suggests, there has not been a significant change in some of the key forms of parliamentary activity that reflect parliament's decisional functions or its role as a channel for pressure groups' demands. While attempts are being made to make institutions less permeable, they have yet to close off a number of access points available to interest groups.

THE BUDGETARY PROCESS

Italy's struggles with trying to bring its public finances under control, especially in light of the convergence criteria of the Maastricht Treaty, are well known and have been described elsewhere.[18] The budgetary process can provide some insight into the ways in which the fragmented nature of decision making that has characterised most of the period since the mid-1970s has provided incentives for interest groups both to target parliament and to use legislators as channels for their demands.

Italy did not adopt a cohesive, comprehensive budgetary procedure until 1978. Prior to the reform introduced that year, government spending and revenues were determined by bills introduced throughout the year. This made it extremely difficult to keep government spending under control and for any sort of planning. The only check was Article 81 of the constitution, which states that all expenditures must indicate the source of funding; more often than not, this provision was either ignored or public sector borrowing provided financial cover for deficits. This meant that interest groups could mobilise around individual bills that may not have attracted the attention of spending or revenue measures contained in a broad, comprehensive budget. The bills could be deliberated upon in committee or, if they did come to a vote in the assembly, they were likely to be decided upon by secret ballot. Clearly, there was little central control over the public purse-strings, thereby providing sectional interests with ample opportunities to target legislators.

The haphazard approach to the budget faced great challenges as spending commitments grew throughout the 1970s; commitments that were partly seen as the result of sectional interests being able to capture parts of the budgetary process in parliament. Reforms were introduced in 1978 that aimed to rationalise the budgetary process by, amongst other mechanisms, consolidating spending and revenue measures into one legislative provision.[19] Members of the legislature would now have to consider a single bill that contained all the financial commitments for the year. However, this did not lead to a rationalisation of the process and pressure groups could continue to see opportunities to influence budgetary decisions. As David Hine has argued, the new procedures created a finance bill that was guaranteed to pass, as failure to approve it would shut down all government operations or have them operate on provisional measures. Under the previous regime, bills as ordinary bills were subject to the difficulties that all measures faced in getting approved by the Italian Parliament. The result was that legislators introduced thousands of amendments to each annual budget because they had a greater likelihood of being accepted in the hope to get the whole budget approved than they would as separate pieces of legislation.[20] The result was that although the government would set targets for levels for spending and revenues, each article and amendment of the bill would be approved separately before voting on the bill as a whole. This meant that legislators were not constrained by limits set by the government; there was, then, an incentive for lobbyists to continue to pressurise members to promote their interests. One important change in the 1980s was to the voting procedures on the budget. Members now vote on the general lines of the budget, including spending and deficit targets, before considering individual articles and amendments in the bill. There remain a great number of amendments that are added to the bill but these now can only operate within the spending limits approved in the general principles.

The budget has been subject to many of the challenges that all government legislation has faced in parliament: negotiation on the timetable, little control over the fate of amendments, and the possibility that small groups of members of parliament could mobilise to influence or even change budgetary provisions. The process, especially in the 1980s before measures were taken to put deficit levels to a vote before voting on individual items, contained many features of that found in the United States. The government sets the main contours of the budget; but there is ample space for individual members to define the fine details.

The Italian budgetary process, then, has been an open process that has allowed space for both insider and outsider groups. The high profile insider groups are able to gain privileged access to the government well before the budget arrives in parliament. Trade unions and employers' associations have been central partners in the search to address public finance problems by restructuring the welfare state. In the search for an agreement, parliament is essentially marginal. Negotiations take place primarily through the Prime Minister and the relevant ministries; and interest groups make use of the media and extra-parliamentary forms of pressure, such as protest and strikes, to influence policy outcomes.

However, the highly permeable budgetary process in parliament leaves great room for sectional interests to craft parts of the budget to respond to their demands. Numerous committees consider parts of the budget, and any number of amendments that alter the government's plan may be added at this stage. If pressure groups fail here, they can still hope for success on the floor of the assembly where rejected amendments may be reintroduced. Moreover, even small groups of legislators can mobilise to delay or obstruct passage so that some consideration must be given to their demands. Pressure groups, then, have a number of entry points into the process. It is not surprising, therefore, that Italy had problems with keeping deficit levels under control in the 1990s, and that all reforms that are being considered aim to reduce the permeability of the process.

CONCLUSION

The eleventh legislature (1992–94) will be remembered less for having enacted some of the most severe budget cuts in Italy's post-war history than for having over 200 senators and deputies indicted on charges of corruption or accepting illegal funding from private interests. The fact that some of Italy's leading industrialists were involved in many of these charges is an indication that the fine line between lobbying to promote private interests and carrying out parliamentary duties had been crossed. It also might indicate that private interests saw that there were opportunities to shape policy decisions in parliament. Unfortunately, this form of pressure group activity has masked the many ways in which interest groups interact with parliament to influence policy.

The case of the Italian Parliament indicates that the capacity to affect decisions will shape the ways in which pressure groups direct their efforts to achieve desired results. Parliament retains the capacity to affect decisions, and, therefore, is a target for pressure groups. One of the problems facing policy making in Italy is that there are too many targets, both within and outside parliament. The multiplicity creates not only incoherence and uncertainty in decision making; it raises broader questions about transparency and accountability for decisions.

Yet, the story is not entirely bleak. The fact that parliament is attractive to pressure groups has helped the legislature develop many of its information-gathering mechanisms. This has strengthened its capacity of oversight of the executive, and has often put the representative institution at the centre of the national political stage. It has helped counter the image of parliament captured by special interests. Parliamentary bodies such as the Budget Committee of the Chamber have assumed an influential and respected role in the attempt to have Italy meet the convergence criteria for EMU. Parliament's access to pressure groups has often allowed it to fill a vacuum left by a weak political and administrative executive. The challenges that Italy faces is how to give greater clarity and coherence to its decision-making structures and processes without diminishing parliament's capacity to gather information, influence policy and maintain links with civil society through pressure groups.

NOTES

1. W. Grant, *Pressure Groups, Politics and Democracy in Britain* (Hemel Hempstead: Philip Allan, 1989), pp.14–21.
2. For instance, see J. La Palombara, *Interest Groups in Italian Politics* (Princeton: Princeton University Press, 1964); M. Regini, 'Social Pacts in Italy', in I. Scholten (ed.), *Political Stability and Neo-corporatism in Italy* (London: Sage, 1987).
3. M. Regini, 'Relazioni industriali e sistema politico: l'evoluzione recente e le prospettive degli anni '80', in M. Carrieri and P. Perulli (eds.), *Il teorema sindacale* (Bologna: Il Mulino, 1985).
4. M. Regini and I. Regalia, 'Employers, Unions and the State: The Resurgence of Concertation in Italy?', in M. Bull and M. Rhodes (eds.), *Crisis and Transition in Italian Politics* (London and Portland, OR: Frank Cass, 1997).
5. A. Chiesi and A. Martinelli, 'The Representation of Business Interests as a Mechanism of Social Regulation', in Peter Lange and Marino Regini (eds.), *State, Market and Social Regulation* (Cambridge: Cambridge University Press, 1989).
6. G. Pasquino, 'Rappresentanza degli interessi, attivita' di lobby e processi decisionali: Il caso italiano di istituzioni permeabili', *Stato e mercato* (Dec. 1987), pp.403–29.
7. D. Hine, *Governing Italy: The Politics of Bargained Pluralism* (Oxford: Clarendon Press, 1993), pp.1–10.
8. See A. Manzella, *Il Parlamento*, 2nd edn. (Bologna: Il Mulino, 1992).
9. G. Di Palma, *Surviving Without Governing* (Berkeley: University of California Press, 1977).
10. For instance, see M. Ruffolo, 'Una Finanziaria a perdere: Manca il numero legale, lobbisti all'assalto', *La Repubblica*, 7 Dec. 1991, p.17.
11. For a more detailed discussion, see V. Della Sala, 'The Italian Parliament: Chambers in a Crumbling House', P. Norton (ed.), *Parliaments and Governments in Western Europe* (London and Portland, OR: Frank Cass, 1998).
12. Della Sala, 'The Italian Parliament'.
13. A. Caporale, 'Spendete, spendete, una lobby paghera', *La Repubblica*, 25 Jan. 1992, p.6.
14. It led one of Italy's leading constitutional experts to ask whether there was a

government in Italy. See S. Cassese, *Esiste un governo in Italia?* (Roma: Officina Edizioni, 1980).
15. Camera dei Deputati. XII Legislatura. *Atti Parlamentari: Discussioni.* 7 Feb. 1995. Rome.
16. For a more detailed discussion of the various activities of parliamentary committees, see Della Sala, 'The Italian Parliament'.
17. L. Verzichelli, 'Gli Eletti', *Rivista Italiana di Scienza Politica*, Vol.24, No.3 (1994), pp.717–19.
18. V. Della Sala, 'Hollowing Out and Hardening the State: European Integration and the Italian Economy', *West European Politics*, Vol.20, No.1 (Jan. 1997), pp.15–33.
19. See P. De Ionna, 'Dalla legge n.468 del 1978 alla legge n.362 del 1988: Note sul primo decennio di applicazione della legge finanziario', *Quaderni Costituzionali*, Vol.9, No.2 (1989), pp.110–25.
20. Hine, *Governing Italy*, p.185

CHAPTER 5

Belgium: Insider Pressure Groups in an Outsider Parliament

LIEVEN DE WINTER

Belgium is often presented as a strong case of partitocracy. In this degenerated form of party government, political party organisations not only control the process of selection of the top political personnel and decide on general government policy,[1] they also control recruitment in the wider public sector, the judiciary, public media and lower echelons of the executive and interfere regularly and directly with decision making in these sectors.[2] Parliament evidently does not escape from partitocratic dominion. Parties fully control the recruitment of MPs, as the voters only decide on the number of seats each party gets. Strong discipline and a battery of measures to enforce it assure the government the permanent support of MPs of the majority coalition parties. Hence, parliament's role in government formation, oversight and legislation is marginal.[3] In this partitocratic vision, pressure groups, like other formal and informal political actors (government, parliament, the civil service, the judiciary and the media) play only a marginal or complementary role in the decision-making process.

The neo-corporatism and pillarisation approach to Belgian politics puts pressure groups much more in the foreground, although not ignoring party dominance. Neo-corporatist visions[4] point to the importance of pressure groups in government decision making, through a well developed set of several hundred formal advisory and co-decisional bodies, in which groups are consulted and often participate in the decision making and even the implementation process, with the government playing the role of conductor, third party, arbiter or mere rubberstamp. Once pressure groups and the government have reached an agreement[5] parliament's role is limited to its formal ratification.[6] In addition to this formal neo-corporatist network, an extensive and often occult network of informal negotiations seems to operate.[7] Clearly, these consultative and (co-)decisional networks undermine parliament's and the executive's competence in many policy sectors whereby the former ratifies and the latter executes decisions taken in the neo-corporatist network.[8]

The importance of these pressure groups is related to the consociational or pillarised character of Belgian society. In fact, the predominance of political parties, or at least the traditional ones (Christian Democrats, Socialists and Liberals) is partly due to the fact that they aggregate, articulate, defend and implement the interests of a wider network of organisations that are constituent elements of a 'pillar', 'societal segment' or 'sociological world' and which include trade unions, farmer and 'middle class' organisations, socio-cultural organisations, educational and health service networks, and press networks.[9] Their strength is due to the fact that the policy implementation in many sectors of public life (such as public health, education, social security and family help) is to some extent subcontracted to pillar organisations. These constituent parts of the system of segmented pluralism have gradually grown into political concerns, oligopolies or conglomerates that to a large extent monopolise the access of civil society to the political system.[10]

With three out of four workers, employees and civil servants members of a trade union, Belgium has one of the highest degrees of syndicalisation in the world.[11] The strongest trade union in terms of membership and votes in social elections is the Christian Democratic trade union, with about half of all trade union members; the Socialist trade unions represent four out of ten. The second most influential groups are the health mutual insurance organisations (*mutualités*). The Christian ones represent nearly half of all citizens which fall under this system, against only a little over a quarter for the Socialist *mutualités*. Third, in the socio-medical sector, more than half of the hospitals are associated with the Catholic pillar. Catholic organisations also have a predominant (and usually majoritarian) position in the sectors of retreat houses for the aged, the disabled, homes for juvenile readaptation, family consultancy centres, home medical care, family and aged care, socio-cultural organisations and youth organisations. In the politically sensitive sector of education, 70 per cent of the Flemish school and university-going population goes to Catholic institutions, and half of the Walloon.[12] In short, in most sectors of social life, one finds a few, ideologically competitive and – taken together – quite representative pressure groups, with strong links to the traditional political parties. Hence, in terms of Grant's classification, the pressure groups that are most influential in the Belgian polity are those that fall under the high and low profile insiders category. Yet, some insider pressure groups are less strongly pillarised: the employers' organisations, the medical professional associations and other liberal professions.

Although often MPs hold leadership positions in these pillar organisations, are sponsored by them and therefore act as representatives not only of their party, but also as spokepersons for the specific interests of adjacent pillar organisations, these groups predominantly exert their influence through direct contacts and bargaining with the executive. Parliament is only a secondary focus of lobbying, probably even less important than political party headquarters and the media.[13]

But it seems that outsider groups also do not focus much on parliament. Although the literature on pressure groups and (new) social movements is not abundant, the existing empirical studies do not mention extensive lobbying of MPs as one of their main strategies.[14] This is probably due to the fact that parliament is generally rather insensitive to direct pressure exercised by non-institutionalised groups, as MPs of the traditional parties are generally insensitive to direct pressure from groups not belonging to their pillar.[15]

Therefore, this chapter mainly focuses on the relation between (pillarised) insider pressure groups and parliament. This relationship, although rather marginal in terms of policy impact, is stronger in some sectors than in others.[16] It has also evolved over time, and so has the role of government.[17]

The impact of insider pressure groups on parliament operates through a variety of channels and mechanisms. First, they not only constitute an interesting recruitment reservoir for parties looking for socially embedded candidates, they also participate actively in the candidate selection process. Second, also after their election, MPs sometimes remain active pressure group leaders and/or behave as pressure group representatives. Third, pressure group interests seem to be important in choosing committee membership and subject of specialisation and affect MPs' behaviour inside and outside parliament. Pressure groups also add to MPs' resources.

The impact of these insider pressure groups on governmental and parliamentary decision making has been increasingly criticised, further delegitimising parliament and representative democracy. However, this critique also opens a perspective of a 'pluralist' parliament more accessible to a wider variety of less well entrenched interests, and therefore more responsive to shifts in public opinion.

PRESSURE GROUPS AND CANDIDATE SELECTION

Pressure Groups as Recruitment Reservoirs
Pressure group office holders traditionally represented an important recruitment reservoir for MPs. Debuyst found that, in 1964, four out of ten MPs of the traditional parties had held a leadership position in a socio-economic pressure group before becoming an MP (of which two-thirds held it in an organisation linked to the workers' movement, and one-third to employers' organisations).[18] Our survey of the early 1980s showed that of the most prominent occupations held by members of the House of Representatives (in their entire pre-legislative occupational career), pressure group offices come second to educational occupations.[19]

More recent data suggest that pressure groups still constitute a prominent recruitment reservoir.[20] Table 5.1 presents the percentage of MPs that either held a position in different recruitment reservoirs at the moment of the survey (1996) or did so in the past. It shows that – apart from holding a local, regional or national party office – leadership offices in socio-economic pressure groups (trade unions, business organisations and professional organisations) constitute an experience in the past shared by more than four out of ten representatives and

TABLE 5.1
CURRENT AND PAST EXPERIENCE IN ORGANISATIONS
(percentages of respondents holding/held office in 1996 survey)

	House		Senate	
	Current	Past	Current	Past
Local/regional party	72.2	20.7	68.5	25.8
National party	48.3	25.9	66.7	12.1
Professional organisation	5.9	16.5	8.2	22.7
Trade union	7.3	19.9	0.0	14.7
Business organisation	6.6	6.4	9.2	5.2
Women's organisation	7.1	4.9	23.7	3.3
Environmental group	5.7	8.3	8.6	14.6
Religious organisation	5.3	7.7	4.6	6.1

senators. However, most MPs give up these activities upon becoming MPs. Leadership positions in non-economic groups (women, environment or spiritual organisations) have been held and are still held by one out of five MPs.[21]

Pressure Groups as Candidate Selectors

Pressure groups not only offer an attractive recruitment reservoir from which parties can pick skilled and visible candidates, in some parties they are actively involved in the candidate selection process. The role of pressure groups in candidate selection has always been, and still is, most visible in the Flemish Christian Democratic party, the CVP. As this party constitutes the largest and pivotal party in the highly fragmented Belgian party system,[22] and it has since 1958 been always in government and nearly always provided the Prime Minister, we will examine this case more closely than the other main governing parties.

Christian-Democrats. The CVP is a Flemish Catholic catch-all party which appeals to Catholic workers, farmers, and 'middle classes' (that is, shopkeepers, artisans, liberal professions and entrepreneurs). These three socio-economic categories are highly organised, and, together with the Catholic educational network, health sector and cultural and leisure organisations, constitute the most influential Catholic 'pillar'. All these bodies consider the CVP as the sole political representative of their interests. All three have active sections at the constituency level and are represented as *standen* (estates) in the local and constituency parties. Each tries to achieve as much power within the party as possible. Control over the selection of political personnel at all levels – local, constituency, provincial and national – is a major part of their strategy of power achievement.[23] Constituency party leaders strive to compose electoral lists that will not alienate these interest groups and their followers. Usually, delegates of the three interest groups in the constituency party committee come to an agreement regarding safe places that they can reserve for their own candidates.[24]

Thus, nearly all CVP MPs obtained their seats because one of the *standen* offered them a safe place on an electoral list. Most of these groups organise regular meetings between their MPs and the leadership of the groups at the federal and constituency level, where MPs are briefed about the issues at stake in parliament and the party that are dear to the estates. These estates will also ensure that their MPs become members of the committees that are relevant to the estates' interests.

In the PSC, the smaller French-speaking Christian-Democratic party, socio-economic interest groups are less well organised at the constituency party level. In addition, many changes occurred in the institutionalised representation of the three social categories within the party framework. In 1983, after destructive clashes between the conservative and workers' wing that menaced the survival of the party, all organised factions were formally prohibited. Since then, the representation of socio-economic pressure groups in the PSC occurs through informal, less institutionalised contacts. Still, for most elected and party offices, a fair distribution between the factions remains the norm.[25] Apart from MPs with informal links with the socio-economic pillar organisations, one finds a large number of *sans famille*, that is, without formal or informal links to these organisations.

Socialists. Also the Socialist pillar harbours a large number of pressure groups, but they are less competitive than their Christian-democratic colleagues, as nearly all belong to the socialist workers movement. Socialist MPs are often member of all or most important Socialist pillar groups, such as the trade union, the health organisation, cultural organisation and co-operatives. Until the end of the 1970s, party statutes imposed group membership as an eligibility requirement.[26] By now, due to the danger of pillar inbreeding that these stringent eligibility conditions tend to bring, requiring a total integration of a candidate – and of his or her family – into all organisations of the Socialist pillar, these conditions have been weakened considerably and even dropped by most (or at least the Flemish) constituency parties.

Still, until the introduction of the public financing of parties in the beginning of the 1990s,[27] Socialist trade unions and health insurance organisations often financially supported the electoral campaigns of particular candidates, as these organisations constitute the financial backbone of the Socialist movement. Also, leaders of the trade union and health care organisations can mobilise their rank-and-file members, and even their personnel (for which party membership is often required), to vote for them in the 'poll', the intra-party primary elections.[28]

Liberals. The Liberal pillar is clearly the weakest in terms of organisation, membership and integration of the pillar with the party organisation. Still, in some constituencies, organisations of the Liberal pillar traditionally played a prominent role in the selection process (especially the Liberal health insurance organisation) often through the form of a reserved eligible place on the candidate list for candidates representing a pillar organisation.

Since the 1990s, the link between liberal pillar pressure groups and the Flemish Liberals has been further eroded, given the party leadership's campaign against pillarisation and neo-corporatism in the Belgian polity. The new party statutes make the mandate of the pressure group official incompatible with an elected office.

Other parties. In the other parties, pressure groups hardly interfere with candidate selection and internal decision making, as the Green Ecolo-Agalev, the Flemish-nationalist Volksunie and extreme right Vlaams Blok are not the political voices of a pillar. In fact, these parties have always been quite critical of pillarisation and neo-corporatism. The Volksunie and the Greens even prohibit their members from combining their elected and party office with offices in pressure groups.

Yet, even in these parties MPs are encouraged to cultivate informal links with different types of pressure groups and social movements. These links with civil society are taken into account in candidate selection as well as the committee assignment process, as involvement in such networks not only boosts an MP's electoral value, but also enhances the member's specialisation and expertise in committee subject matters.

STRUCTURAL OPPORTUNITIES FOR PRESSURE GROUP INFLUENCE ON PARLIAMENT

In spite of the overwhelming constraints of partitocratic government for pressure groups to play a significant role in the decision-making process, the structure of the Belgian Parliament does offer some structural opportunities for interest group representation.

First there is the committee structure: committees in both chambers are specialised, permanent and compact in number[29] and membership.[30] Membership is also rather stable, as most parliamentary groups allocate membership on the basis of seniority and MPs' special links with the policy sector, including with organisations representing the interests of these sectors.[31] Hence, the number of parliamentary decision makers in a policy field of interest to particular pressure groups is rather small and stable.[32] However, the extreme fragmentation of the Belgian party system, which – as proportionality is the rule – is reflected in the committee composition, complicates the exercise of influence. While, before the end of the 1960s, it sufficed for pressure groups to lobby some MPs of two governing parties in order to mobilise a winning majority in their favour, now they have to convince MPs of at least twice as many parliamentary groups.

Until 1985, all committee meetings were held behind closed doors. This facilitated the unrestrained expression by committee members of the viewpoints of their sponsoring pressure groups. Since 1985, the House has started experimenting with opening some committee meetings to the public. Since the 1993 statutory reforms, as a rule all the permanent policy committee meetings are open to the public, unless decided otherwise. Still that does not mean that pressure groups can openly interfere with committee proceedings. Although committees can – in order to prepare their legislative work – gather advice and ask for documentation of persons or institutions not belonging to parliament, the number of hearings remains extremely low.[33]

This structure suggests that committees may not be bodies really representative of the entire House, but rather stacked with MPs serving special interests operating in the policy sector of the committee.[34] In fact, committee members are usually 'outliers' *vis-à-vis* the entire House, serving the interest of the groups and social categories they represent or the interests of local governments in which they hold office. In a strong legislature with a high degree of specialisation, this situation would lead to policy-segmented or even corporatist decision making and biased policy outputs. Yet, given the strong impact of the executive over parliament in general, but also in matters discussed and decided within committees, the danger for 'unrepresentative' decision making by outlier committees is less acute.[35]

The main role of committees in the Belgian Parliament is the passage of legislation, including budget bills. MPs formally have quite large legislative competencies in terms of initiation of private members' bills and amendments to government bills In fact, the number of bills has grown steadily in the post-war period to nearly 500 a year in the late 1990s.[36] Although government bills get priority treatment in the committees, and therefore many private members' bills never get discussed, MPs can amend bills at this stage, as well as in the final plenary reading of the bill. Often, amendments that failed in committee are pursued in the plenary, showing to MPs' client groups that they tried to defend their particular interests.

Also, MPs' tools for controlling the executive can and are often used to serve particular group interests. Interpellations of ministers, the classical and most powerful tool of parliamentary control, usually aim at obtaining information from the government or criticising governmental actions. Although, in principle, matters of local or special interest are excluded, in practice these tend to be more numerous, and there has been a steady growth in their use (from around 40 a year in the 1950s to more than 500 in the late 1990s). Given the particularistic nature of many interpellations, the House increasingly tends to relegate them to public committee meetings. Only interpellations of general or exceptional political importance are still held in the plenary session.

The different types of parliamentary questions can also be

used to serve special interests. They can demand clarification or confirmation, aim at exposing a neglect, abuse or bad application of the law, and sometimes suggest improvements and reform. Also, their number has steadily increased: at the end of the 1990s more than 3,000 written questions a year are being asked, and nearly 500 oral and urgent questions. As about half the questions only concern demands for information and are often inspired by mere electoral and publicity-seeking motives,[37] these questions can provide written proof that MPs have taken to heart a matter raised by constituents or client pressure groups.[38]

The current set of ineligibility and incompatibility rules does not prohibit the combination of a parliamentary mandate and that of a pressure group office holder. Neither do MPs have to declare their links with particular pressure groups. However, MPs who have exercised important leadership functions in such groups as their main profession tend to mention this in the official *Biographical Notes* and other biographical publications. Therefore, in their legislative or control activities, they do not have to declare the interests they may be serving. Until now, they have not had to declare outside income either, although the principle of a non-public register of members' outside earnings and personal wealth was approved in 1997 (but probably will become effective only in 2000). Pressure groups or lobbyists do not have to register either. Hence, the political exchange between MPs and pressure groups can go largely unnoticed in the public arena.

PRESSURE GROUPS AS RESOURCES FOR MPs

Pressure groups' sponsorship and office holding usually provide important resources relevant to MPs' intra- and extra-parliamentary work.

Material Resources
The Belgian Parliament is characterised by scarce institutionally provided resources. The House has only 492 permanent employees, of which only about a quarter have a university degree. Of those with degrees, only three dozen (those working for the Service for Studies, Documentation, Statistics and Archives and the Library of Parliament) are available to offer

intellectual assistance to individual MPs. The Judicial Service – with limited staff – can assist individual legislators in the technical problems of drafting a private member's bill. Each committee has one assistant, who provides committee members with documentation. Apart from these services, no collectively provided staff accessible to individual members are available.

Also in terms of non-institutional staff facilities, resources are limited and relatively recent. Since 1980 each MP has been allocated funds to employ a personal assistant. Given the salary level (that of clerk), these assistants are used mainly for secretarial work, such as correspondence, filing and constituency casework.[39] In 1988, university-trained assistants were allocated to political groups at a proportion of one per eight representatives. By 1995, this had grown to one for each MP. However, most political groups in both chamber and senate pool these staff resources.[40] In some parties, they work exclusively for the parliamentary group, but in most they work for the party research centre or the party organisation at large. Hence, this resource is less of a help to individual MPs than it may seem.

Also in terms of housing, institutional resources are scarce. Until 1987, only a few leading MPs had a personal office in the Palais de la Nation building. Since then, the problem of limited accommodation has been solved through the annexation of a large adjacent building that offers each MP a private office with telephone and fax, and each parliamentary group meeting rooms and offices for their secretariat.[41]

The traditionally poor institutional staffing of individual MPs, and the well-subsidised party research centres add to an MP's dependency on his or her party organisation. MPs often rely on information provided by their party research centre as far as the drafting of bills, amendments and interpellations are concerned. For most policy sectors, a group of paid experts and volunteers define the party's policy positions, in collaboration with the MPs specialised in these fields. Thus specialist MPs are to a large extent dependent on their party's brain trust, as they do not have at their disposal independent staff and information resources, like the research centres of pressure groups. In fact, our survey indicated that in the early 1980s nearly half of backbenchers could rely on the services of pressure groups. Most important socio-economic pressure groups do have relatively large research departments, which not only scrutinise the sector's evolution, but also prepare policy proposals aimed at defending the groups' interests. While most of this activity seems oriented towards the executive, these research centres also assist MPs in drafting bills and amendments, interpellations and parliamentary questions. Sometimes MPs introduce private members' bills that are drafted entirely by these research centres.

Pressure groups can furthermore offer financial support for personal staff, access to secretarial facilities or to specialised information, spacious offices not far from parliament, cover for parliamentary expenses and an additional income. Hence, given their poor institutional staffing, pressure groups constitute one of the channels through which Belgian MPs manage to mobilise additional help from a wide variety of sources, especially with regard to their work inside parliament, and to a lesser degree also for their extra-parliamentary activities.

Political Skills
MPs occupying leadership offices in pressure groups have usually acquired leadership skills that may be useful for the job of an MP. Also, they may already have acquired certain political skills and knowledge in dealing with executive bodies at different levels. They are well acquainted with the demands and problems of the organisation that has sent them to parliament, and, therefore, they know well how to defend the interests of those they represent.

Political Influence
The support of pressure groups is considered by many MPs as one of the instruments for enhancing one's policy impact, as groups can help to mobilise public opinion.[42] Being a (former) leader of an important pressure group will also boost a backbencher's status within the party and towards ministers and the civil service.

Electoral Resources and Candidate Selection
MPs hold pressure group leadership offices also for promoting their political career. First, pressure group office holding is one of the prominent career paths to a seat in parliament, especially for MPs with socio-demographically less

advantageous backgrounds. It can serve as an apprenticeship and a power base for the further political career. In addition, intra-party pressure groups (especially in the CVP) not only control candidate selection but are also used to sponsor the actual election of their candidates in terms of campaign costs contribution; they still promote candidates in their membership periodicals and affiliated newspapers, and offer them a chance to meet the members and activists of the organisation. Finally, in case of non-election, groups can lobby the party to have their candidate 'fished up' as co-opted senator or senior assistant to a minister (in the so-called *cabinet ministériels*), or provide for a fallback cushion within their organisation.

Constituency Service and Visibility
Most MPs hold regular (at least monthly) surgeries in the different communes of their constituencies. These surgeries are usually announced in the local papers and in the local publications of the party and sponsoring pressure group. They are usually held in the backroom of a pub, in the local offices of the party or pressure group and in town hall offices.

Constituency party and pressure group work, local office and casework contribute to strengthening an MP's visibility and notoriety amongst the constituency inhabitants. Constituents want to be represented by somebody they trust as a person, who they see often, who is 'one of them', who is always open to their concerns. This generation of trust usually necessitates face-to-face contacts that increase MPs' chances of being remembered and liked by constituents, and chosen at the next ballot.

MPs attend a wide variety of meetings and social gatherings organised by a wide variety of local and constituency organisations, groups and institutions, such as chambers of commerce and trade unions, pensioners, cultural, sports, youth or women's organisations, and local government boards. This 'local notable' or even 'flower pot' role includes inaugurating buildings, distributing prizes, making dedications, opening commercial and cultural initiatives, attending festivities, balls, receptions, sports manifestations, fancy fairs, even funerals and weddings. Belgian MPs have ample opportunities to participate in community life, as the distance between the capital and the constituency is for most MPs less than an hour's drive and most

MPs tend to go their constituency home every evening. Pressure groups therefore constitute a prominent channel for meeting and serving the constituency, and being seen to do so.[43]

MPs AS PRESSURE GROUP REPRESENTATIVES

Privileged links with pressure groups can affect the behaviour of individual MPs in several ways. First, there is the combination of a parliamentary mandate with a pressure group office. Second, MPs may see representation of pressure groups as their main role orientation. Third, pressure group links seem to affect specialisation and committee membership. However, pressure groups seem to be marginal as sources of voting cues. Finally, pressure group membership and leadership seems to affect MPs' activities inside parliament.

Cumulation of Offices
In comparison with previous inquiries,[44] the involvement of representatives in pressure groups and other organisations of civil society has declined considerably over the last two decades.[45] In fact, our first survey indicated that in 1980 the average backbencher held 6.2 leadership positions in pressure groups, especially in the culture and leisure sector, the social and health sector, the mixed economy sector, education and science, socio-economic pressure groups, and finance, commerce and industry. Our 1996 survey indicates that pressure group leadership offices are still held in quite different sectors, but now by only a small number of MPs (see Table 1).[46]

Representational Focus and Cue-Taking
Our 1980s survey revealed that Belgian MPs see themselves as representatives of socio-economic and demographic categories and their organisations (like workers, farmers, middle classes, often defined nation-wide), of linguistic communities and regions (Walloons, Flemings, Francophones and so on), of denominational groups (Catholics and freethinkers), and as representatives of their party and their voters at different levels. Thus, MPs consider themselves representatives not only of their party, but also spokespersons for the specific interests of adjacent pillar organisations that organise these categories.

Yet, as far as voting cue taking is concerned, the 1980s survey suggests that the interference of the constituency party, pressure and action groups, and public opinion must all yield to national party voting cues,[47] given the party-disciplined nature of voting in the Belgian Parliament. Hence, in general, intra-party factionalism, ideological disputes or conflicts concerning territorial interests very rarely manifest themselves in voting rebellions within a parliamentary group.[48] Also, when facing conflicting expectations between party and pressure groups, most MPs follow the party opinion.[49]

Parliamentary Behaviour of Pressure Group Representatives and Leaders
As representatives of pressure groups, MPs are expected to defend the policy interests of their sponsors within the legislature, within the party and towards public opinion. Thus, interest group representatives tend to specialise in the subjects that are of concern to their representational focus. In fact, our survey indicates that specialisation in a specific field is primarily the product of external factors: previous occupation, personal interest and experiences, while also constituency, local office and pressure group interests are at its roots. The importance of the policy field for the sponsoring pressure group is in fact mentioned by nearly four out of ten MPs in the 1980s survey.[50]

In addition, they seek membership of and leadership positions in committees that are dealing with policy matters relevant to their sponsoring interest group, constituency or commune. In fact, nearly one out of every five MPs claimed pressure group interests as their main reason for preferring a particular committee.

In these committees, they initiate and monitor relevant legislative proposals and amendments or oppose harmful legislation or amendments. In plenary sessions, they secure their group's interest by speaking in debates, asking parliamentary questions, or intervening in the government's budget. Our survey does indicate that pressure group members attend committee and plenary meetings more assiduously than the average MP.

However, MPs that combine their elected mandate with a pressure group office tend to be generally less active in the plenary assembly, as their additional office sometimes absorbs considerable time. In addition, pressure group leaders have other and more powerful means of controlling the executive at their disposal, through direct formal and informal contacts in the neo-corporatist arena.

Interest group leaders also tend to sit on the committees which deal with the policy sectors of their interests, and as a result have additional opportunities for controlling the minister responsible for these sectors. In fact, they tend to be more active committee members (in terms of attendance and time budget), and spend more time in preparation of parliamentary work, as committee proposals and budgets have to be carefully scrutinised and alternatives formulated on behalf of the pressure group. They are also more active in committee reporting, as they will seek to be committee rapporteur of the proposals that affect their group, in order to protect its interests.

CONCLUSION

Belgian MPs nurture good contacts and even occupy a wide variety of leadership positions in different types of pressure groups, organisations and institutions, usually in those linked to their own pillar. This office holding is supportive to the political career and provides influence and resources that the mandate in itself does not provide. The structural organisation of the Belgian Parliament also offers ample opportunities for pressure group representation.

Still, in spite of the existence of powerful and well-organised pressure groups with large followings and well embedded in the party system, their impact on parliamentary decision making is marginal. This is due to the overwhelming predominance of political parties in the decision-making process. In the Belgian partitocracy a large proportion of decisions affecting interest groups are taken outside parliament, in the executive–party nexus and the neo-corporatist decision-making arena. Given the relative irrelevance of parliament, most influential pressure groups directly contact members of the government, and the leaders, executives and the research centres of the governing parties, but rarely MPs or the chair of the parliamentary party.[51] Recent research on the organisation and functioning of parliamentary parties in the House reveals that although most parliamentary parties are contacted occasionally by pressure groups, the latter usually address parliamentary parties as the last resort, when other strategies have failed.[52] Hence, pressure groups will first lobby the ministers and their personal staff (*cabinet ministériel*) and the party leadership (president and executive bureau). In addition, in most parties the hearing of pressure groups has been institutionalised in the party research centres, where representatives of pillar organisations work together in research groups with party experts and MPs at the preparation of legislative proposals, and where other groups are heard as well. Hence, parliament is not the focus of pressure groups' lobbying activities, although the latter are well represented in terms of political personnel.

Still, the current wave of criticism of pillarisation and neo-corporatism opens some opportunities for enhancing the hitherto weak position of parliament in the Belgian decision-making process and increasing its legitimacy.[53] Yet, this empowering of parliament and MPs is seen to require a reduction of the impact of pressure groups on the selection of political personnel and on the decision-making process, inside and outside the parliamentary arena. The current attempts at drafting deontological codes regulating MP–lobbyist relations, as well as the recent introduction of incompatibility rules between pressure group and political offices in the statutes of some parties, indicate that the politically rather insignificant relationship between parliament and pressure groups may be eroded further.

NOTES

1. R.S. Katz, 'Party Government and its Alternatives', in R.S. Katz (ed.), *Party Government: European and American Experience* (Berlin: De Gruyter, 1987), pp.1–26.
2. K. Deschouwer, L. De Winter and D. Della Porta (eds.), 'Partitocracies between Crises and Reform: The Cases of Italy and Belgium', Special Issue, *Res Publica*, Vol.48 (1996).
3. L. De Winter, 'Parliament and Government in Belgium: Prisoners of Particracy', in P. Norton (ed.), *Parliaments and Governments in Western Europe* (London and Portland, OR: Frank Cass, 1998); L. De Winter, A. Timmermans and P. Dumont, 'Belgien: über Regierungsabkommen, Evangelisten, Gläubige und Häretiker', in W.C. Müller and K. Strom (eds.), *Koalitionsregierungen in Westeuropa* (Bildung, Arbeitsweise und Beendigung, Wien, Zentrums für angewandte Politiek-

forschung, 1997), pp.371–442.
4. For an analysis of the neo-corporatist decision-making process in Belgium and the relation between pressure groups and MPs, see Y. Nuyens, *Pressiegroepen in België. Een benaderend onderzoek* (dissertation, Leuven: Instituut voor Politieke Wetenschappen, 1965); P. Claeys, *Groupes de pression en Belgique. Les groupes interm,diaires socio-économiques. Contribution à l'analyse comparative* (Bruxelles: Editions de l'ULB, 1973); A. Van Den Brande, 'Neo-corporatisme en functioneel integrale macht', *Tijdschrift voor Sociale Wetenschappen*, Vol.25 (1980), pp.33–60; X. Mabille, 'a concertation sociale: crise du système belge', *Pouvoirs*, No.54 (1990); A. Vanderstraeten, 'Neo-corporatisme en het Belgisch sociaal-economisch overlegsysteem', *Res Publica*, Vol.28 (1986), pp.671–88; W. Dewachter, *Besluitvorming in Politiek België* (Leuven: Acco, 1992); and the special issue of *Res Publica*, Vol.37, No.1 (1995).
5. Trade unions and employers organisations had by 1991 concluded nearly 30,000 social agreements, of which 9,813 were in formally constituted 'parity committees' at the sector level. A. Pernot, 'Formele en informele overlegstructuren', *Arbeidsblad*, No.1 (1992). Since 1968, these agreements have been legally binding.
6. In some cases, social agreements render obsolete laws voted by parliament. For instance, in 1981, the social partners concluded an agreement that neutralised a law voted by parliament that was passed in order to put the social partners under pressure to arrive at an agreement. For a long time, agreements among the main socio-economic pressure groups were regarded as being as binding as laws. However, following the economic recession of the 1970s, agreements between different groups became more difficult to achieve, which enhanced the active role of the government in most traditionally 'corporate' policy sectors.
7. Pernot, 'Formele en informele overlegstructuren'. During the early 1980s, the Christian-Democratic PM Martens and his *chef de cabinet* regularly spent weekends with two leaders of the Christian trade union movement at the *chef*'s bungalow in the Ardennes. During these meetings it was decided how far the centre-right government could go with its stringent measures for budgetary and economic recovery without losing the support of the trade union, that is, the strongest faction within the Christian-Democratic family. These talks were only revealed in 1991. H. De Ridder, *Omtrent Wilfried Martens* (Tielt: Lannoo, 1991), pp.145–64.
8. Dewachter, *Besluitvorming in Politiek België*, pp.138–9.
9. For a general analysis of the features of pillarisation in Belgium, see L. Huyse, *De verzuiling voorbij* (Leuven: Kritak, 1987).
10. Huyse, *De verzuiling voorbij*.
11. E. Arcq, 'Le taux de syndicalisation 1982–1991', *Courrier Hebdomadaire du CRISP*, No.1386 (1993).
12. Most Catholic pillar organisations managed to keep up their organisational strength and membership in spite of the decreasing church participation and deconfessionalisation of the public at large by enhancing the service character of their organisations and by somewhat deconfessionalising their activities at the grass-roots level. The organisations of the other pillars have also softened their ideological identity. See Huyse, *De verzuiling voorbij*.
13. L. De Winter and P. Dumont, 'The Belgian Party System(s) on the Eve of Disintegration', in D. Broughton and M. Donovan (eds.), *Changing Party Systems in Western Europe* (London: Cassell, 1998).
14. See, for instance, S. Hellemans, *Nieuwkomers of het middenveld*, *Res Publica*, Vol.35, No.2 (1993), pp.197–211; S. Hellemans and M. Hooghe, *Van Mei '68 tot Hand in Hand* (Leuven: Garant, 1995); M. Hooghe, *Nieuwkomers of het middenveld* (Ph.D.

thesis, Vrije Universiteit Brussel, 1997); and S. Walgrave, *Tussen loyauteit en selectiviteit. Een sociologisch onderzoek naar de ambivalente houding tussen nieuwe sociale bewegingen en groene partij in Vlaanderen* (Ph.D. thesis, Leuven: Departement Sociologie, 1995).

15. According to Hooghe, *Nieuwkomers of het middenveld*, p.379, the Belgian political elites follow a strategy of publicly ignoring new social movements, while, on the other hand, the issues of such movements rather easily make it to the agenda of political parties and the government. Hellemans, *Nieuwkomers of het middenveld*, explains the fact of the continuing predominance of traditional pillar organisations and parties by their capacity of integrating demands (and to some extent the activists) of these new social movements into their own agenda and organisation. Hence, the direct impact of these movements on the decision-making process remains marginal.
16. Therefore, in comparative perspective, Belgium constitutes a case situated in the middle of the span of corporatism. A. Lijphart and M. Crepaz, 'Corporatism and Consensus Democracy in Eighteen Countries. Conceptual and Empirical Linkages', *British Journal of Political Research*, Vol.21 (1991), pp.235–46.
17. A. Vanderstraeten, 'Neo-corporatisme en het Belgisch sociaal-economisch overlegsysteem', in D. Luyten (ed.), *Sociaal-economisch overleg in België sedert 1918* (Brussels: VUB Press, 1995). Binding decision-making involving neo-corporatist actors is the strongest in the sector of labour conditions, wages, employment and wage-replacing income (pensions, unemployment benefits, transfers) and public health. As far as economic planning is concerned, pressure group–state relations are basically restricted to consultation, while the financial sector generally escapes from neo-corporatist consultations. The role of the government varies between involved partner, binding or voluntary arbiter and inspirator. In periods of economic growth, more ambitious and detailed agreements are concluded at the national level, while since the 1980s only more modest agreements, at the level of the industrial sectors or of individual enterprises only, have been concluded. In addition, some of the formally designated consultative and co-decisional bodies have been leading a marginal life, or have been bypassed by informal or *ad-hoc* meetings.
18. F. Debuyst, *La fonction parlementaire en belgique. Mécanismes d'accès et images* (Bruxelles: CRISP, 1967), p.115.
19. L. De Winter, *The Belgian Legislator* (Ph.D. thesis, Florence: European University Institute, 1992). This type of occupational background is overrepresented amongst Christian Democratic MPs, followed by the Socialists, and finally the Liberals. These differences correspond to the width and the degree of organisation of these three pillars.
20. L. De Winter and M. Brans, 'Professional Politics in a Partitocracy in Crisis', in J. Borchert (ed.), *Politics as a Vocation* (Oxford: Oxford University Press, 1998). The written postal questionnaire of the 1996 survey on Political Representation in Europe included a closed-end question on the political background of MPs. Our 1982–83 survey used a different question technique, therefore straight comparisons over time are not feasible.
21. Nearly one out of every four senators currently exercise a function in a women's organisation. This difference is mainly due to the better representation of women in the senate and the importance of these organisations for the political career of female politicians.
22. Rae's index of fragmentation reaches 0.88 since the last two general elections. L. De Winter and P. Dumont, 'Belgium: Subjects of Partitocratic Dominion', in K. Heidar and R. Koole (eds.), *Behind Closed Doors: Parliamentary Party Groups in European Democracies* (London: Routledge, 1998).

23. J. Smits, 'Les standen dans les partis sociaux-chrétiens', *Courrier Hebdomadaire du CRISP,* Nos.1134–5 (1986).
24. In most constituencies a long lasting agreement (one that is valid for many elections) has been reached. As a result, in the 1965–95 period, the trade union wing managed to get nearly half of the parliamentary seats, the agricultural faction about one out of six, the middle class faction just over one out of five, leaving about one out of ten mandates to the *sans famille*. Smits, 'Les standen dans les partis sociaux-chrétiens', and J. Smits, 'Tussen partij en beweging: de CVP van 1968 tot 1995', in W. Dewachter *et al.* (eds.), *Tussen Staat en Maatschappij. 1945–1995 Christen-Democratie in België* (Tielt: Lannoo, 1995), p.161. These *estateless* CVP MPs are usually national party leaders or cabinet members, with a strong electoral appeal and intra-party power. They cannot be neglected in the bargaining process between the groups and are tolerated by the estates on safe places on the list.
25. Y. Georges, 'Les tribulations existentielles du parti social chrétien', in P. Delwit, P and J.-M. De Waele (eds.), *Les partis politiques en Belgique* (Bruxelles: Institut de Sociologie, 1997), pp.83–102.
26. Most constituency party charters require a minimal party membership of five years, membership of the Socialist trade union and Socialist health insurance fund of five years minimum. In addition, some constituencies' charters require membership in the Socialist co-operative and annual minimum purchases, subscription to the party newspaper, the holding of a party office, the enrolling of children in state rather than private (that is, Catholic) schools, a high level of party activity, that private insurance be held through the Socialist insurance company, membership of spouse in the party, the trade union and the medical insurance fund, and membership of children in party youth organisations! J. Ceuleers, 'De verrruimingsgedachte in de BSP: de lokale weerstanden', *De Nieuwe Maand*, Vol.23 (1978), pp.36–40.
27. D. Van Bunder, *De officiële inkomsten van de politieke partijen en hun parlementaire fracties* (Vrije Unviersiteit Brussel: Centrum voor Politicologie, 1993).
28. L. De Winter, 'Belgium: Democracy or Oligarchy?', in M. Gallagher and M. Marsh (eds.), *Candidate Selection in Comparative Perspective: The Secret Garden of Politics* (London: Sage, 1988), pp.20–46.
29. The number of permanent committees varies over time. With the reduction of the size of the House from 212 to 150 seats and the Senate from 186 to 71 in 1995, their number has been reduced to ten in the House and six in the Senate. In addition, there are a number of quasi-permanent committees with specific tasks, some advisory committees and one bicameral conference committee. In addition to the permanent committees, one usually finds for each legislative term a few *ad-hoc* committees, created in order to solve a specific matter at a given moment of time. De Winter, 'Parliament and Government in Belgium', in Norton (ed.), *Parliaments and Governments in Western Europe*.
30. Most permanent House and Senate committees count respectively 17 and 15 permanent members.
31. De Winter and Dumont, 'The Belgian Party System(s) on the Eve of Disintegration'.
32. On the other hand, the turnover of MPs seems to have declined considerably, which undermines committee membership stability. Fiers calculated the overall average seniority at 9.0 years for representatives in the 1946–92 period. After the 1995 elections, the average number of years of parliamentary experience was only 5.51 years for the House, while after the 1978 elections the incumbency of representatives was still 7.7 years. De Winter, *The Belgian Legislator*, p.201.
33. The permanent House committee all taken together held only a dozen hearings

with private interests in the entire 1995–96 session. Chambre des Représentants de Belgique, *Rapport Annuel. Session Extraordinaire 1995. Session Ordinaire 1995–1996* (Bruxelles, 1997).
34. For instance, in the Committee for the Interior, which covers the department most central to local government, more than 90 per cent of members are local office holders. M. Jennar, 'Le parlement: une institution en crise', *Courrier Hebdomadaire du CRISP*, Nos.1013–14 (1983). Likewise, representatives of the trade unions are overrepresented in Social Affairs, Infrastructure and Health Committees, members of the Farmers' Union and the Christian Middle Class Association are overrepresented in Agriculture and Economy Committees, representatives of the *mutualités* in Health and Social Affairs Committees, and so on.
35. However, the ministerial departments are also 'colonised' by special interest representatives, especially by the CVP-*standen*. L. De Winter, 'Parties and Policy in Belgium', *European Journal for Political Research*, Vol.17 (1989), pp.707–30.
36. De Winter, 'Parliament and Government in Belgium', in Norton (ed.), *Parliaments and Governments in Western Europe.*.
37. F. Drion, 'Les questions parlementaires ècrites', *Res Publica*, Vol.17 (1975), pp.201–22.
38. MPs can also voice pressure group opinions in regular debates. Debate can occur on nearly every matter raised by the government in parliament. Often, plenary debate is used for attracting media attention to the main points MPs already made in committee sessions, and offer an opportunity for the opposition to challenge ministers.
39. De Winter, *The Belgian Legislator*.
40. De Winter and Dumont, 'The Belgian Party System(s) on the Eve of Disintegration'.
41. De Winter and Brans, 'Professional Politics in a Partitocracy in Crisis'.
42. Asking pressure groups to intervene with ministers is mentioned by one out of ten MPs as a useful strategy to influence decision making. De Winter, *The Belgian Legislator*.
43. In fact, our survey indicates that pressure group office holders tend to be more active in constituency and local party work. As pressure group leadership positions are often held at the level of the constituency, they are slightly more active in the constituency social life, that largely takes place inside the organisations of the pillar of which the pressure group is part. De Winter, *The Belgian Legislator*.
44. H. De Bondt, *Stratificatie van de Belgische Parlementsleden bij middel van hun extraparlementaire bindingen* (MA thesis, Leuven: Departement Politieke Wetenschappen, 1971); M. Ronsmans, *De cumulatie van mandaten door de Belgische parlementsleden* (MA thesis, Leuven: KUL Departement Politieke Wetenschappen, 1985).
45. Although that study covered a larger number of offices and organisations. But even for the sector of socio-economic pressure groups we arrived at an average of 0.7 positions per MP, which is clearly much more than the 1996 figures for trade unions, business and professional organisations taken together. De Winter, *The Belgian Legislator*, p.326.
46. Also, those that in 1996 held a leadership position in a pressure group spent less time on it (on average only 2.1 hours weekly in 1996, against 3.4 hours in 1980). The time spent by MPs on nursing contacts with pressure groups in which they do not hold a leadership offices has remained the same, that is, about one and a quarter hours. De Winter, *The Belgian Legislator*, p.326. This evolution suggests a further increase of professionalisation, as the office of MP becomes more and

BELGIUM

more detached from other positions.
47. De Winter, *The Belgian Legislator*.
48. For the 1954–65 period, Langerwerf calculated that, as far as legislative proposals and amendments originating from the Cabinet or the House are concerned, on average only 1.14 per cent of representatives voted differently from the rest of their parliamentary group. E. Langerwerf, 'Het stemgedrag in het parlement. Onderzoek in de Kamer van Volksvertegenwoordigers voor de periode 1954-1965', *Res Publica*, Vol.22 (1980), pp.177–88. Verminck found similarly high degrees of party cohesion for 1985. M. Verminck, 'Consensus en oppositie in het Belgisch parlement tijdens een verkiezingsjaar', *Res Publica*, Vol.28 (1986), pp.475–87. In the entire post-war period, in each chamber, on the average only 0.6 per cent of majority MPs voted against the government at the investiture vote. L. De Winter, A. Timmermans and P. Dumont, 'Belgien: über Regierungsabkommen, Evangelisten, Gläubige und Häretiker', in W.C. Müller and K. Strom (eds.), *Koalitionsregierungen in Westeuropa* (Bildung, Arbeitsweise und Beendigung, Wien, Zentrums für angewandte Politiekforschung, 1997), pp.371–442.
49. Nearly all pressure group representatives had experienced this type of role conflict. In nearly six out of ten cases of conflict, the pressure group representative decided to follow the party's position. Less than one out of ten stuck to the position of the pressure group. However, in a majority of cases, the MP managed to avoid the difficult choice between the role of party or pressure group representative, in the first place because party and pressure group came eventually to a compromise, and – to a lesser extent – by circumventing the choice for either one of them by abstaining or not voting.
50. De Winter, *The Belgian Legislator*.
51. The 1986 IAO survey indicated that three out of four MPs believed that the social partners exert their influence directly on the executive, and two out of three thought they did so on the political parties. Hence, MPs do not feel they constitute a privileged focus of pressure group attention. When asked where most important decision are taken, parliament comes last (first comes inside parties, between parties, between ministers, inside lobbies and in corporatist concertation).
52. De Winter and Dumont, 'The Belgian Party System(s) on the Eve of Disintegration'.
53. Nearly three out of four Belgians believe elected representatives have lost contact with their voters. De Winter, 'Belgium: Democracy or Oligarchy?' Six out of ten do not have trust in the honesty and competence of parliamentarians. *Studie naar het vertrouwen dat de Belgische bevolking heeft in de eerlijkheid en bekwaamheid van een aantal (overheids) organisaties en maatschappelijke sleutelfiguren* (Antwerpen: IMADI, 1989), p.60. The latest Eurobarometer (No.47.1) showed that, of the 15 EU countries, Belgians are the least satisfied with the functioning of democracy, and have the lowest degree of confidence in political institutions and political establishment.

CHAPTER 6

The Netherlands: Parliamentary Parties Rival with Pressure Groups

M.P.C.M. VAN SCHENDELEN

Pressure groups are by definition interest groups which try to influence the outcomes of political decision making. Like water streaming into the basement of structures, they seek to find the places of political power and to tie the power holders. Does this happen in The Netherlands *vis-à-vis* the national parliament? Is its constitutionally powerful Lower House (second chamber or *Tweede Kamer*) an important target of pressure group activities? The paradoxical answer for the present is no. The pressure groups go mainly to different and, in particular, administrative holders and structures of power. The parties-in-parliament recently adopted a policy intended to restrict this. The parties rival the pressure groups; basically, the voters rival the citizens. The Dutch paradox will be described and analysed in the context of systemic change.

1917–60: PILLARISED GROUPS RUN THE PARLIAMENT

Up to the end of the 1960s, the Dutch political system was widely described as a consociation of socio-political pillars: the Catholics, Protestants, Socialists and Conservatives lived inside their own infrastructure (pillar) of family networks, schools, housing corporations, hospitals, mass media, interest groups, political parties, voluntary associations and so forth. Loyalty and interaction were high inside the pillar and extremely low between the pillars. This system of organised *apartheid* was formed around 1917 when the four groups settled the issues of general suffrage, private schooling and class inequality.[1]

Every group has always remained a minority, covering 20 to 30 per cent of the population. The election law of extreme proportional representation, in itself a compromise of accommodation, miniaturised the divided society at the level of parliament. Cabinet formation, usually based on a standing parliamentary majority, became identical to coalition formation. In theory, the state could have been governed by the cabinet and its majority in parliament. In practice the mutual distrust between the pillars and their parties-in-parliament prevented the development of strong central government.

Instead of this there developed a practice of highly informal elite accommodation at two levels. Inside each pillar the leaders (foremen) of the various interest groups negotiated and settled their disputes, for example, between their organisations of employers and the employed. On issues beyond their reach, for which they needed support from other pillars or the government, they subsequently formulated their pillar's position. Their common interest, however, was to keep the number of these issues as low as possible, that is, to accord the pillars maximum independence in rule making and implementation. Where necessary, they tried to accommodate the inter-pillar disputes in informal and secret meetings, with their deferential adherents at distance.

This practice had important consequences for parliament. For informal and secret negotiations, the parliament – with its more or less public nature – was clearly not the best place. Negotiations usually took place elsewhere: in restaurants, in semi-autonomous (and sometimes corporatist) government bodies and agencies, in all kinds of offices and even abroad. The parliament was used as a podium for rank-and-file mobilisation and, as far as the government had to be involved, as a procedure to formalise and legitimise the negotiated compromises. To safeguard that formalisation, usually by legislation, and to control the government's implementation, the foremen of the pillars wanted to have a seat in parliament. This was particularly the case with the second chamber, with its strong powers of legislative initiative, amendment and approval and of parliamentary control as well; the First, or Upper, House (*Eerste*

Kamer) has no such powers. A parliamentary majority was formed composed of leading figures from the major pillar-related interest groups, such as those of the retailers, the employed, the employers, the farmers, the mass media or the universities. These groups tended to get safe seats (so-called quality seats) on the party lists of candidates. The elected usually kept their seats for many years, so becoming very experienced MPs. As part-time politicians they also kept their positions in their organisations, as a result directly linking their interest groups to the parliamentary party.[2]

In short, until the end of the 1960s the major interest groups tended to have, through their related party, a seat in parliament. The majority of MPs was composed of interest group representatives. They participated in the meetings for both intra- and inter-pillar negotiations, which normally took place outside parliament. In the parliament they could safeguard the compromises which needed government action.

THE TRANSITION, CIRCA 1970: PARTIES TAKE OVER THE PARLIAMENT

By the mid-1960s two new developments in Dutch society became manifest and interrelated. The one is the growth of central government, the other the decline of pillarisation.

More and more the foremen of the pillars had to meet the rising expectations of their rank-and-file, particularly in the domains of social welfare (social security, housing, health and education). Their problem was finance. They chose to solve the problem not by collecting more money from their pillarised people, but by burdening the government's budget. To do this they had easy access by the way of their representatives in the parliament. Their privately run welfare organisations became publicly financed and improved; other sections, such as the farmers and the retailers, were not forgotten. Later than in other west European countries, but at a higher speed, Dutch central government was built up.[3] Its public spending, volume of legislation and number of civil servants (and likewise other public employees, as in education) exploded to proportions unparalleled in surrounding countries. The budget, legal rights and important administrative positions were equally distributed among the pillars and their interest groups.

Almost at the same time the pillarised structures of society began to be questioned at the grass-roots. Younger people especially left the old pillar structures and began to enjoy a 'different' school, newspaper or sports club. They eschewed deference for the foremen and instead became critical of their political style of informal and secret wheeling and dealing. They asked for transparency and public accountability. They showed dislike of depoliticised compromises and wanted to politicise social issues. They also discarded the old culture of passivity and became highly active in social movements, public action groups and new political parties.[4] For them, the existence of an expanded and still expanding central government was a matter of course. By-passing the elites of the old pillars, they demanded from the government new procedures, new structures, new policies and new personalities. They hoped to get rid of the old pillars.

The years between the mid-1960s and the mid-1970s can be seen as a period of transition. Dutch society sharply reacted against the old beliefs and structures. At the social level, all sorts of organisations (such as universities, trade unions, hospitals and local administrations) were the focus of critical debate and had to change their old practices and personnel. New social movements and interest groups mushroomed. The hinge of the transition, however, turned out to be the political parties. In their manifestos and their lists of candidates they soon adapted to the new popular demands. They channelled most of the social turbulence.

Two reasons can be given for this crucial role of the parties. The first is that they, being directly dependent on popular (electoral) support, were among the first organisations to feel the new winds blowing coldly and turbulently. In a few years the parties of the Catholics and the Protestants lost up to 30 per cent of their electoral support. Per election the net-shift of parliamentary seats between the parties more than doubled to 13 per cent of all seats. New parties were formed. The party system fragmented, with small parties tripling their share of seats, up to almost one-third of the (directly elected) second chamber. The parties, in short, had no choice than to react rapidly and sharply. The second reason is that the parties, thanks to the election law, possessed the key to parliament, forming the cabinet that runs central government. They had not only the willingness, but also the legal capacity to transform the political system.

The second chamber rapidly changed in its functioning; the (indirectly elected and less powerful) first chamber remained almost unaffected. For the general public the second chamber became the major platform of articulation of values and public debate. Competition among the parliamentary parties to (re)gain popular support intensified and led to polarised and lengthy (even nightly) debates. Cabinet stability was permanently in danger. Much political energy was invested in keeping alive or destroying the sitting cabinet. More and more the tone in parliament was set by a multitude of mainly young and inexperienced new members, who were free from the old values and got the chance to express their views thanks to an increased turnover of MPs (measured from election to election) which more than tripled to about half the membership. They came mainly from government-related sectors, such as public administration and social welfare organisations, particularly education.[5] The majority of MPs, once recruited from pillarised interest groups, soon possessed this background. They produced an unprecedented activism, be it measured by numbers of parliamentary questions, motions, interpellations, amendments or committee sessions.[6]

There was also organisational change within the second chamber. In 1968 MPs got much better salaries and reimbursements, allowing them to function full-time and independently of interest groups. For the chamber, the parties and the individual MPs more staff were made available. The system of parliamentary committees became more institutionalised and achieved special importance in combination with the growing practice of the (larger) parties to divide the parliamentary work among all their MPs. So-called party specialists were born. To the party they acted as cue givers for the plenary meetings, so replacing the old dominance of the leader(s) of the parliamentary party. In their related committees they found a formal position and status and were able to negotiate with the specialists from other parties.[7]

Dutch pressure groups reacted differently, according to their political fortunes. Some survived the transition, as did the farmers' organisations in the Christian parties and the trade unions in the Socialist party. The unions even strengthened their parliamentary position under the socialist-led cabinet of 1973–77. Some new not-for-profit pressure groups, closely related to social movements, took advantage of the transition and got parliamentary support or even position, for example, the pressure groups on disarmament, consumer protection and the environment.

But the majority of profit-oriented pressure groups were disappointed and critical. They lost positions in the political parties and parliament. They attracted the odium of having been the lifeline of the old establishment and the old values. Leading party specialists in the chamber disliked their participation in negotiations. The sideline activities of MPs, particularly in profit organisations, came under negative public debate and subject to voluntary registration a few years later (1976). The introduction of an unprecedented delegation law by the new Socialist-led cabinet in 1973, to control prices, became the breakpoint between the cabinet and its parliamentary majority on the one side and organised business on the other. The major employers' organisation (VNO) gave voice to the criticisms from business. Having lost their pillarised position in parliament, the business pressure groups had no choice other than to become politically entrepreneurial. The VNO started to professionalise itself into a lobby organisation in 1973. Other trade organisations and business umbrella organisations took advantage of depillarisation and joined forces. Finding themselves unwelcome in parliament, they tried to approach public administration directly.

1970–90: A COMBINATION OF ADMINISTRATION AND PRESSURE GROUPS

Pillarisation not only stimulated the formation of a rich variety of pressure groups, but also gave them a foot in the public administrative system. The government budget, legal rights and higher administrative positions were carefully and equally distributed among the various pillars and their interest groups. For example, the Christian school organisations were intimate with the Ministry of Education, the farmers with that of Agriculture, the trade unions with the Ministry of Social Affairs and organised business with Economic Affairs. For some policy fields, such as agriculture and retail business, corporatist structures have been made by government law, which entitled representatives from the trade unions, the employers' organisations and the dominant political parties (so-called independents) to run the sector by the way of public law. With the growth of central government, the pillarised pressure groups automatically collected more of the budget, more legal rights and more positions inside. More and more they nestled in the bureaux of government administration.

During the transitional years, many new MPs had the ambition to make central government independent of most of the old pillarised pressure groups. But for two reasons they did not gain effective control over central government. One factor was their legalistic belief in delegated legislation. Believing that their span of direct control was inadequate, they increasingly approved the delegation of legislative powers to the cabinet and, essentially, to the administration (ministries and agencies). The second factor was party political instability, which consumed much of their energy and attention. The electorate remained highly unpredictable in its voting behaviour. All political parties became very uncertain about their next electoral performance and most began to lose party members. Their relationships in parliament remained antagonistic and polarised, especially after the fall of the Socialist-led cabinet in 1977 and the formation of a right-wing cabinet. Cabinet stability remained permanently in danger. The years 1981–82 produced four cabinets and two elections.

With the growth of government, public administration achieved a much greater role in Dutch society. Thanks to the two aforementioned factors it also enjoyed more formal (delegated) powers and more room to manoeuvre, at a distance from politicians. Survey research among electors and MPs in the mid-1970s shows that higher civil servants were considered to belong to the top five most influential players in national decision making.[8]

In many policy fields the relationship between administrative bureaux and pressure groups became intimate and closed off to outsiders (*verkokering*). The two developed into policy communities, combining common policy interests. For their policy making and implementation, the bureaux welcomed information and support from pressure groups. From their side, these groups applied for benign administrative allocations of budget, rights and positions. From now on, they saw the administration as more relevant and amenable to negotiation than parliament was. Thanks to the delegation of powers and the discretionary powers exercised by government, the bulk of decisions in fact came to be made inside the administration. Even when the final decision was formally made elsewhere, the die of decision making tended to be cast here. The exceptions to this pattern were the (usually few) highly politicised issues on which the politicians wanted (but often failed) to make the decision. Civil servants and pressure group representatives felt they had a common interest in not politicising issues, in keeping a low profile and in closing off their policy community so that politicians and countervailing pressure groups could be kept at a distance.

Parliament hardly offered such comparative advantages. Even the trade unions, for long protected by leading parliamentary parties, began to see parliament as less relevant and more risky. Party specialists often appeared to be ineffective in delivering their part of a deal. Issues in their hands ran a high risk of politicisation. Interest groups more and more limited their pressures on MPs to issues which they wanted to push on the political agenda or on which they feared an unfavourable decision, in short, for which they needed politicisation. In daily practice, they were weakly organised groups, the losers inside a policy arena or the neglected outsiders. Profit-oriented pressure groups, being publicly despised by leading politicians, felt the least inclined to go to parliament and were happy with civil servants.[9]

These groups from organised business gave birth, at the end of the 1970s, to an Anglo-Saxon style of lobbying: more professional, operating at an early stage, well prepared, highly informal, with a low profile and reliable in their dealings with administrators.[10] Some big companies and trade organisations were the first to set up small offices in the national capital. Others followed. Negotiating with civil servants, they kept an eye on the risky parliament. The administrative bureaux, already located in the capital, began to develop modern practices of lobbying as well. They developed into public pressure groups of a not-for-profit character. To safeguard their budgets, powers and positions and to realise their policy objectives, they could not rely on solely official procedures of decision making and had to make use of new and informal methods and techniques of lobbying, both inside the government and in the society at large.

This development more or less closed policy communities, consisting of lobbying administrative bureaus and affiliated pressure groups, with parliament at a distance, continued during the 1980s. Some change, however, came from three new factors, all stimulated by the economic recession around 1980. The 1982 elections brought a new type of cabinet, with nine of the 14 ministers having a business background. It launched a programme of privatisation, deregulation, budget savings, de-bureaucratisation and more. Although its results remained for long more rhetorical than substantial, it still expressed a positive reappraisal of profit-oriented pressure groups. Secondly, parliament became more positive with regard to profit-oriented pressure groups and more critical of private not-for-profit ones, such as the trade unions, environmentalists and social welfare groups. The MPs also became less negative about side activities in business organisations and some openly confessed to playing a role as lobbyist for business interests. The third factor is the Single European Act of 1987 and the related Open Market 1992 programme. These resulted in much of the power of government decision making moving from The Hague to Brussels and many private and public pressure groups, profit-oriented or not, followed this shift of power, leaving the Dutch Parliament behind.

THE 1990s: PARLIAMENT WANTS TO REGAIN POWER
OVER THE TRIAD

In the past two decades the parliamentary parties have been confronted with two causes of instability: the electorate and the cabinet. The first problem continues. Party membership dropped in the 1990s to an unparalleled level: less than three per cent of the electorate.[11] In the 1994 elections support for the three major parties (Christian, Socialist, Conservative) dropped from above 80 per cent in the 1980s to 66 per cent, about ten per cent less than in the transitional years. New parties (for aged persons and leftist radicals) entered the scene. The net shift of seats in the second chamber reached 23 per cent.

The second problem, cabinet instability, was more or less effectively solved by the cabinet and the coalition parties. Through written agreements (*regeeraccoorden*), weekly informal meetings, personal management by the Prime Minister, parliamentary party control of the party specialists and a rigid whip system the subsequent cabinets remained (with a minor exception) in the saddle. More and more the cabinet got a grip on both the parliament and the administration. It got from parliament the legislation it wanted and, particularly through the Ministry of Finance, pushed by the plan for European Monetary Union, it broke open some parts of the closed administrative policy bureaux.

Confronted with increasing electoral instability, the political parties again changed their manifestos, lists of candidates, promises and teams. In the new second chamber of 1994 roughly half the members were new. The large majority again came from government-related sectors. Having a weak link of representation with the population and confronted with a cabinet that dominated the legislative process, the new second chamber more and more voiced the ambition to achieve control of central government. The tone was set by the first chamber, which in the early 1990s became more critical of cabinet proposals and policies. A 1990 survey among MPs shows that in the second chamber there was growing criticism of the dominant roles of public administration, 'Brussels' and pressure groups.[12] The ambition to achieve parliamentary government even got an old ideological label: *the primacy of politics*, that is, the elected politicians should run the state through their control of the cabinet.

The general indicator of the new ambition is the explosion of parliamentary investigations: from a yearly average of 0.4 during 1946–90 and 1.8 in the years 1990–94 to 3.5 in the first two years of the new second chamber. Parliament supported cabinet proposals to create a general civil service for higher administrative positions, to diminish the number of civil servants, to decentralise some bureaux and to turn others into independent agencies, all in order to make the administration more flexible, effective and controlled. To improve parliamentary control of 'Brussels', a set of new procedures to make the cabinet more accountable was adopted.[13] As regards pressure groups, in 1996, at the instigation of a special parliamentary commission, parliament adopted the so-called Desert Act (*Woestijnwet*), ordering that the approximately 100 official advisory bodies, composed of all sorts of pressure groups, be reduced (with two exceptions) to one per ministry.[14]

The effectiveness of all this new parliamentary activism, driven by the belief in 'the primacy of politics', remains to be seen. The many investigations have certainly created unrest and caution within the administration, but not necessarily produced behaviour compliant to the wishes of parliament. Some measures of the administration are more symbolic than substantial, such as the creation of a general civil service and the reduction of civil servants (replaced by commercial labour), while others even limit the effectiveness of parliamentary control, for example, decentralisation of power to provincial and local authorities and the establishment of agencies which are legally independent. The many new procedures covering 'Brussels' certainly produce more paper and information, but so far have not had a greater impact on ministers and civil servants acting in committees of the Commission, working groups of the Council or in the Council itself.[15] And the Desert Act, covering pressure groups, reflects a misunderstanding of their behaviour: it will only stimulate more informal lobbying, as is shown already by the use of new labels for old practices. For example, administrators and pressure groups now meet in steering groups, panels or institutes.

Yet most pressure groups behave differently than before, albeit not in line with the wishes of parliament. Many more pressure groups than before now invest in professional lobbying of administrative bureaux and, increasingly, of crucial role players in Brussels. They include not only private pressure groups, being profit-oriented (as companies) or not-for-profit (as trade unions and environmentalists), but also the public ones of the government itself, with a profit-orientation (as public transport) or without (bureaux and local authorities). They use parliament primarily for the limited objectives of politicisation (pushing an issue or preventing an unkind decision). They show little affection for MPs and almost no interest in providing jobs for the many ex-MPs. The main change of their behaviour, however, comes from the Brussels-inspired government programmes to reduce the budget, to deregulate and to privatise. The pressure groups have now at least the expectation that budget resources, legal rights and favourable positions are scarce. They also feel that the administrative bureaux have less to offer. Driven by this scarcity, most players now want to intervene in the many other policy communities, formerly closed but now bursting open. One effect is that these combines develop into more open and competitive arenas, entered by a variety of bureaux and groups. Unintentionally, they bring more coherence and balance into central government. Another effect is that the cabinet, having to compromise between competing ministries, is in a stronger position. The old segmented combines are, in short, now being transformed into a broader and more comprehensive triad. But the parliament still remains at a distance.

CONCLUSION

Parliament, defined as an *institution*, had the strongest position during the years of pillarisation, when it in fact was composed of pressure group representatives. Since these groups were expelled from parliament (transitional period) or self-reliantly found administrative channels to get their demands realised (afterwards), they reduced parliament to a procedure for either rubber-stamping decision making or politicisation of issues not won elsewhere. But parliament defined as a collection of elected *politicians* had at least an authentic position during the transitional years, and in its most recent years, when it wanted and again wants to regain power. An authentic parliament, however, is not identical to a powerful one. After the transitional years, the combines and, later on, the triad of administration, pressure groups and cabinet, operating both at home and in Brussels, possessed the real power. Unless MPs get an effective grip on cabinet, as their Trojan horse inside the triad, a change in their power position is not probable.

Constitutionally, the Dutch political system is ruled by parliament. The current MPs also believe in the primacy of (their) politics. But a constitution is a norm, not necessarily a reality.

And the parliament, as a collection of MPs, has only a weak and highly unstable linkage with society: that is, through political parties which are in decline. The pressure groups have much stronger roots in society. As long as the political parties want to have the political primacy by the way of parliament, and as long as their MPs want to keep the pressure groups at distance, they will continue to marginalise the power of parliament as an institution. As soon as they re-open their party manifestos and lists of candidates to accommodate the many pressure groups, they may restore the power of parliament as during the period of pillarisation, but at the cost of their own position. The old question remains: who should run parliament? The political parties or the pressure groups? The voters or the citizens?

NOTES

1. A. Lijphart, *The Politics of Accommodation* (Berkeley, CA: University of California Press, 1968). See also M.P.C.M. van Schendelen, 'Consociational Democracy: The Views of Arend Lijphart and Collected Criticisms', *Political Science Reviewer*, Vol.15 (1985), p.143–84; K. Gladdish, *Governing from the Centre: Politics and Policy-Making in the Netherlands* (London: Hurst, 1991); R. Andeweg and G. Irwin, *Dutch Government and Politics* (London: Macmillan, 1993).
2. J.Th.J. van den Berg, *De toegang tot het Binnenhof* (Weesp: Van Holkema en Warendorf, 1983), chapter 5.
3. M.P.C.M. van Schendelen and R.J. Jackson (eds.), *The Politicization of Business in Western Europe*, 2nd edn. (London: Routledge, 1990), chapter 4.
4. Sociaal en Cultureel Planbureau, *Sociaal en cultureel rapport* (Den Haag: Staatsuitgeverij/VUGA, bi-annual since 1974) provides data.
5. Van den Berg, chapter 5; on turnover P. de Vos, *De uitgang van het Binnenhof* (Arnhem: Gouda Quint, 1990), providing results of exit-interviews.
6. M.P.C.M. van Schendelen and V. Herman, 'On Legislatures and Societal Change', *Acta Politica*, 17 (1982), pp.205–30.
7. M.P.C.M. van Schendelen, 'Information and Decisionmaking in the Dutch Parliament', *Legislative Studies Quarterly*, 31 (1996), pp.499–523.
8. G. Irwin *et al.*, *Codeboek Nationaal Verkiezingsonderzoek 1977* (Leiden: Political Science Department, 1978) variables 366–79; S. Eldersveld *et al.*, *Elite Images of Dutch Politics* (Ann Arbor, MI: University of Michigan Press, 1981), p.204.
9. M.P.C.M. van Schendelen *et al.*, 'Leden van de Staten-Generaal, ...' (Den Haag: VUGA, 1981), chapter 12; M.P.C.M. van Schendelen, *Codebook The Dutch Member of Parliament 1979–80* (Rotterdam: Political Science Department, 1981), variables 421–30.
10. J. Louwerse and H. Commandeur, 'Business Techniques of Lobbying' (in Dutch), *Namens*, 3 (1988), pp.25–9.
11. R. Katz and P. Mair (eds.), *Party Organizations* (London: Sage, 1992).
12. J.J.A. Thomassen *et al.*, *De geachte afgevaardigde* (Muiderberg: Coutinho, 1992), chapter 9.
13. M.P.C.M. van Schendelen, 'The Netherlands: From Founding Father to

THE NETHERLANDS

Mounding Baby', *Journal of Legislative Studies*, Vol.3, No.1 (1995), pp.60–73.
14. Document of the Second Chamber: TK 24.232. Of related interest are TK 23.725 and TK 24
15. R. Pedler and G. Schaefer (eds.), *Shaping European Law and Policy: The Role of Committees and Comitology in the Political Process* (Maastricht: EIPA, 1996), chapter 2.

CHAPTER 7

Parliaments and Pressure Groups: The Irish Experience of Change

EUNAN O'HALPIN AND EILEEN CONNOLLY

The past three decades have seen a proliferation of organised interest and pressure groups operating within the Irish policy system. There has also been a marked growth in visible interaction between pressure groups and the Oireachtas – the bicameral legislature, in which the directly elected Dail predominates over the upper house or Seanad – and between such groups and individual politicians, both TDs (members of the Dail) and senators (members of the Seanad).

Since 1977, there have been developments in the pattern of electoral politics and of government formation, with increasing voter apathy and coalition governments becoming the norm, which on the face of it suggest a weakening of the stranglehold of the major political parties on public affairs: none of the last seven general elections have produced a single-party majority government. There has instead been just one minority government (1989–92) and six coalitions, of which the current Ahern administration is dependent on independent TDs for a majority. Since 1992, the coalition formation and management process has been marked by unprecedentedly detailed pre-nuptial agreements on policy between the parties, and especially in the 1992 and 1994 coalitions by careful inter-party arrangements for the continuous review of policy.[1] Opinion poll and other data suggest that the voter volatility evident in recent elections will continue, and that coalitions are likely to remain the dominant form of government for the forseeable future. This trend is paralleled by a steady decline in turnout in recent general elections, as voter 'disenchantment and indifference' appear to have grown independently of other barometers of national well-being, such as economic conditions: at 66 per cent, the turnout in the 1997 general election was the lowest since 1927.[2] In all, the recent pattern of electoral behaviour provides considerable evidence of a growing gulf between the mainstream party system and ordinary people.

It can be argued that these developments strengthen the leverage of small parties and of independents in the Oireachtas in government formation and in the passage of legislation, and consequently represent an increment in the potential power of legislators. In these circumstances individual legislators and the various political parties, however small, should logically remain priority targets for pressure groups seeking to influence public policy. There is ample evidence to show that is indeed happening, as part of an overall strategy by such groups to maximise their influence.

The past three decades have also seen a precipitate decline in the power and influence of the Roman Catholic church as a blocking force in national affairs. Where once the shadow of a bishop's mitre struck fear into even the most courageous Irish politician, clerical disapproval is now a minor badge of honour. From exercising unquestioned hegemony in many areas of public policy, particularly in social – including medical – affairs, the Catholic church is now only one voice among many seeking to influence the direction and pace of change in national life. The church's problems have been accentuated in recent years by a succession of sex scandals, from the unveiling of the teenage son of the colourful and progressive Bishop of Galway to an apparently unending litany of child sexual abuse cases brought against priests and religious brothers: as the country's leading newspaper recently put it, 'if the church ... once prompted reverence, now the reaction is often hostility'.[3] This decline may explain the perceptible softening of the church's stance over the last decade even in policy questions with an obvious moral dimension for Catholics. This was clear in respect of the three referendums intended to clarify the confused constitutional position on abortion rights, information rights and the right to travel held in November 1993, all of which arose from Supreme

Court judgments in respect of a pregnant child rape victim, and also in the run-up to the referendum which eventually permitted divorce in 1996. By contrast with the 1980s, instead of attempting to tell people how to vote, the bishops collectively kicked for touch.[4] The dramatic change in the public moral climate is illustrated by the personal circumstances of the current *taoiseach* (prime minister). Separated from his wife, he has breached the most basic of Catholic taboos by living openly with his partner and personal assistant, yet not a clerical dog has barked. Where traditionalist clerics still bang the crozier, the results appear counter-productive: the recently elected president, Mary McAleese, pilloried during her election campaign for her strong Catholicism, and her one-time role as a constitutional and legal adviser to the Catholic hierarchy, became the darling of the liberal establishment through an ill-judged episcopal attack on her for her politically ecumenical gesture in taking communion at a Protestant service in December 1997.

The Catholic church's travails are the most dramatic illustration of a wider phenomenon. Where once the overt exercise of sectoral influence was largely confined to a few bodies deemed representative of the common good, of organised labour, of farmers, of domestic industry and of professional interests, there are now a myriad of organisations, groups and movements demanding a say in public policy at local, national and European level.

In themselves these developments amply merit discussion, because analysis of them contributes to an understanding of the role of the Oireachtas in the increasingly complex Irish public policy process, and to relations between members of the Oireachtas and the electorate. They also cast some more light on one of the hardy perennials of the Irish political science debate, the phenomenon of localism in Irish parliamentary culture, that is, the long observed preoccupation of TDs with brokerage activities on behalf of their constituents. In reality, however, it is the negative aspects of the relationship of pressure groups to the political system that currently dominate public discussion following three discrete sets of revelations occurring between November 1996 and July 1997. These involved the partial uncovering of the extraordinary financial arrangements of a number of senior politicians. They have occasioned the establishment so far of three judicial tribunals to enquire into aspects of the relationship – if any – between the personal receipt by politicians of financial contributions and support, and partiality or bias in the exercise of public power. These matters have, to date, resulted in the resignation from successive governments of two powerful ministers, Michael Lowry (in December 1996) and Ray Burke (in October 1997), and in the public disgrace of Charles Haughey, taoiseach of four governments between 1979 and 1992, who initially sought to mislead a judicial tribunal and whose eventual and reluctant oral evidence to it was described as in many respects 'unacceptable and untrue'.[5] At the time of writing Mr Haughey has embarked on a constitutional challenge to prevent another tribunal from probing further into his and his family's personal financial affairs during his periods of office as taoiseach. The revelations have also resulted in some re-examination of his involvement, together with that of Burke and of the former taoiseach Albert Reynolds, in the questionable administration of an established 'passport for investment' scheme, and in the empowering of a tribunal to enquire into the contentious recent history of land re-zoning in County Dublin, in which Mr Burke played a part. This means that any worthwhile discussion of pressure groups must now address what has hitherto been a great unmentionable in serious writing on Irish parliamentary affairs, that is, the strong possibility that private money can buy public policy favours. In describing this newly opened and embarrassingly rich seam of material in Irish public life, consolation can be drawn only from the reflection that such developments arguably locate Ireland ever more firmly in the mainstream of European democracies. The substantive question which remains is not whether money might buy influence in Ireland – covert donors evidently think that it can – but rather where to locate Ireland on a diagram of democratic sleaze internationally. In addition, is the apparent Irish tolerance of massive financial impropriety involving senior politicians and business interests entirely *sui generis*?

To place these issues in context, it is necessary briefly to consider developments in the basic framework of national policy formulation, including changes within the Oireachtas designed to enhance the role played by backbenchers in national affairs.

PRESSURE GROUPS AND THE NATIONAL POLICY PROCESS

In its general approach to policy formulation, Ireland has arguably got far more in common with continental social democracies than with her nearest neighbour, where the Thatcher revolution put paid to overt interest group consensus as a pre-requisite to economic reform.[6] A succession of increasingly complex national concordats on pay and on wider economic and social policies agreed with the 'social partners' have been negotiated and operated almost without reference to the Dail. Such understandings remain an imperative of government and, for all the discordant noise sometimes heard off-stage at conferences and rallies, also of the recognised social partners. In the last decade, as the scope of the economic and social policy agreements reached has broadened to include not simply pay rates but taxation, economic development policies and social spending, pressure groups argued not only that their particular concerns were going unheard but that a major opportunity to tackle social issues on a consensual and integrated basis was being lost because only the traditional interest groups were involved in the negotiation process.[7] The most vocal have since been accorded an increasingly important role in such negotiations, and have been largely co-opted into the formal structures of neo-corporatist governance to sit alongside the established interests, as was seen during the 1996 negotiations of 'Partnership 2000', which for the first time included an EU-style 'social pillar' where bodies from the voluntary sector, including both charities and community-based self-help movements as well as groups representing the disabled and the long term unemployed, were formally involved in consultations.[8]

In recent years the European Commission's predeliction, in the name of reducing social exclusion and of increasing the EU's popular legitimacy, for forging direct funding and dialogue links with unelected, non-statutory groups deemed to speak for disadvantaged regions, communities or segments of Irish society – the Leader Programmes operated under the structural funds are an example – has also added to an impression that the Oireachtas is being increasingly by-passed. By this analysis, everyone bar the parliament itself is getting an increasing say in the formulation of policy and in the management of national business.

Pressure group development has been facilitated by an accumulation of factors. Amongst these the most salient are improved levels of education, new attitudes in public service management, the advent of low cost desk-top publishing, the vibrancy of the local press and, since 1989, local radio. Also of importance has been the interaction of many pressure groups with analogous bodies in other countries, and with international pressure groups and movements, for instance, in the areas of women's rights and of enviromental protection, which provide not only exemplars and moral encouragement to Irish activists but well researched data to bolster the case for policies which they favour.[9] The women's movement provides a useful example: the Commission on the Status of Women set up in 1970 received some 40 submissions from individuals, organisations and groups of various kinds; in 1990 its successor, the Second Commission on the Status of Women, established to review the economic, social and legal changes which had occurred in the intervening two decades and to recommend further policy developments, received over 200 submissions, a five-fold increase. Amongst the contributors in 1990 were a range of organisations dealing with issues of sexuality, sexual violence and domestic violence which would have been unmentionable in the moral and political climate of 1970: for example, lengthy submissions were received from Women's Aid, the Cork Lesbian Line Collective and rape crisis centres in Dublin and in Galway, themselves all organisations which would have been inconceivable in 1970.[10] It is, however, important to note that the growth in pressure group politics is not associated exclusively with a drive for social modernisation. Perhaps the tactically most astute campaign of the last 20 years was the 'Pro-Life Campaign' organised by the Pro-Life Amendment Committee (PLAC), the Society for the Protection of the Unborn Child and allied groups in 1981–83. The PLAC first embarrassed the two largest political parties into agreeing in principle to promote an amendment to the constitution banning abortion – the argument being that the existing legal ban could be easily overturned by a capricious court judgment. Disunity within the incoming FitzGerald coalition government in December 1982 saw the opposition, supported by some conscience-stricken government backbenchers, force through a text which broadly met PLAC requirements, but which, the attorney general advised, threatened accepted medical practices and was anyway unworkable. One anti-amendment minister lamented that 'this mess' might have been avoided altogether had there been 'contact and trust' between the two major parties, producing a 'common noncommital stance ... instead of a rush to the cliffs like the Gadarene swine'.[11] The amendment was carried by a margin of two votes to one in the referendum. Its critics, however, were vindicated in 1992, when the Supreme Court held that the amendment in effect permitted abortion in certain circumstances.[12]

What the 1981–83 pro-life amendment campaign showed was less the invincibility of the modernised Catholic right than a deplorable failure of the main political parties to cope with a focused and articulate pressure group. The FitzGerald government bungled again in 1986, when it promoted another amendment to remove the constitutional ban on divorce. Once more, even within the government parties many TDs were embarrassed by the proposal, and sought refuge in silence during the referendum campaign. The result was, to quote one minister, a 'campaign that has been nothing short of lousy and half-hearted', in which the initiative was quickly surrendered to the anti-divorce lobby. Supported by 'immense pressure from the pulpit', these forces won a facile victory.[13] As with the pro-life issue, however, this proved only a temporary success: in 1995, after the legislative groundwork had been properly laid, an amendment permitting divorce was narrowly carried. As one of the icons of the Catholic right sourly remarked at the court, unwisely within the hearing of the press, the 'wife swopping sodomites' and their liberal agenda had finally triumphed.[14]

PRESSURE GROUPS AND THE OIREACHTAS

In spite of the multiplicity of channels of influence now available to pressure groups, the Oireachtas and its members remain an important focus for their activities. The Dail remains a principal channel of interest group attention for the same reasons as apply in other countries – information, access and publicity. A TD has access to insider information, can generate publicity and is also in a position to put pressure on the government or an individual minister by tabling parliamentary questions (in practice, most questions are tabled by members of the opposition, indicating that government backbenchers have internal lines to the administration).[15] In addition to this, government backbenchers have direct access to cabinet ministers through weekly parliamentary party meetings. This contact is a two-way process. It gives backbenchers access to information which may not be generally available, as well as the opportunity to lobby ministers personally and to comment on policy performance. Ministers use these meetings to gauge local public and party opinion on policy initiatives and on the performance of government. Opposition TDs, while they lack this direct line of contact with the administration, have the opportunity to question the taoiseach and ministers through the system of written and oral parliamentary questions. As question time in the Dail is televised it generates more public interest than most other aspects of the Dail's business. Having an issue raised at question time is consequently a guarantee of publicity. This gives pressure groups good reason to lobby the opposition parties, focusing particularly on their front-bench spokespersons. This can be a way of putting additional pressure on the government of the day and it also allows groups to maintain a relationship with all political parties in the event of a change of government.

Two levels of lobbying of parliament are visible. One seeks to influence national policy, the other local or constituency issues. Groups concerned with national policy direct their efforts primarily at the parliamentary parties, particularly the front benches, as well as members of relevant Oireachtas committees. Those concerned with local issues lobby all their TDs on a cross-party basis. While TDs are lobbied by the full range of pressure groups, they are most sensitive to representations that have a constituency resonance, either because these concern a local issue, a national issue with a local dimension, or are simply so emotive as to affect the electoral preferences of a significant number of voters. Individual TDs are therefore most likely to pay most heed to lobbying from, or concerning, their own constituencies.

All the political parties, as well as individual TDs, report receiving a growing amount of material from pressure groups and lobbyists of one kind or another. Much of this is essentially policy junk mail, usually in the form of a statement or information sheet and an accompanying letter. It is clear from recent disclosures that all the parties also receive donations from business and other interests, although no one has yet uncovered an instrumental link between any such contributions and policy or administrative decisions taken by the recipients. The better organised interest groups, such as the Irish Business and Employers Confederation and the Irish Congress of Trade Unions, routinely court members of the Oireachtas through invitations to functions and the like. Such contacts undoubtedly help to legitimate the pressure group concerned, and in the case at least of opposition parties can serve to influence their criticisms of government and their own policy promises to the electorate.[16] Ireland as yet has only a handful of professional lobbyists or public affairs consultants, catering mainly for foreign interests wishing to operate in Ireland, but lobbying politicians and government is an emerging specialisation within established public relations, legal and accountancy firms. Organisations as diverse as the Bank of Ireland, the Garda Representative Association and the Irish Tobacco Manufacturers' Advisory Committee now employ firms to put their case to government and to the Oireachtas. The practice is also growing of firms hiring in people with direct experience of the political world – when the former general secretary of Fianna Fail joined a leading financial institution, the business press explained his appointment explicitly in terms of the political connections and know-how which he could offer.[17]

In Ireland, as in other European states, the perceived marginalisation of the legislature has periodically led to calls for reform designed to make its membership more effective in their parliamentary roles as lawmakers, overseers of the executive and appraisers of policy. While there have since been considerable innovations in Oireachtas procedures and practices, most significantly in the extent and workings of its committee system, the results have been very mixed: backbenchers of all parties still complain that they are excluded from any useful legislative role, and some of the more ambitious experiments undertaken have had to be abandoned or radically curtailed essentially because of legislators' inability or unwillingness to make them work effectively.[18] In the autumn of 1997 the Oireachtas unveiled yet another radical reorganisation of its committee system – the fourth major overhaul in 14 years – in an attempt to reduce demands on legislators' time and to provide a clearer focus and improved administrative and research support for their deliberations. It remains to be seen whether this will do much to make Irish backbenchers more effective parliamentarians, and whether they actually support significant change. What Roy Jenkins writes of the contemporary House of Commons applies with at least equal force to the Dail: members 'want to be ministers or at least opposition front-benchers much more than they want to be legislators'.[19]

The recent record of Oireachtas committees inspires little confidence in the ability of their members to examine issues dispassionately and to separate the wheat from the chaff. It does, however, suggest that, precisely because of their defects, committees offer a good audience for pressure groups anxious both to put their views across and to get some publicity. For example, the Joint Committee on Small Businesses which sat from 1983 to 1987 allowed itself to become largely dependent for research support and topics for inquiry on a unit of the (then) Confederation of Irish Industry, and produced a long succession of reports which were little more than partisan small business wish-lists.[20] On the other hand, it was largely dialogue between the Rape Crisis Centres and the Joint Oireachtas Committee on Women's Rights between 1983 and 1987 that was crucial in bringing about a radical and widely praised reform of the laws on rape.[21] In general, however, committees continue to exhibit considerable credulity when confronted with articulate witnesses and impressive looking data: the Committee on Foreign Affairs first established in 1993 has been roundly criticised for its alarming naivety in its dealings with plausible diplomats and representatives of pressure groups of various kinds.[22] Given the shortage of research and administrative support for Oireachtas committees of all kinds, it is probable that they will remain exceedingly soft targets for any coherent pressure group, however selective its data or outlandish its case, wishing to set the agenda and to influence thinking and ultimately policy.

The increasing influence of pressure groups may be deprecated as sometimes contributing to a naive 'single issue' style of political discourse at the expense of considered analysis. So far as can be judged, however, the public views growing pressure group demands for involvement in policy processes as entirely legitimate, and as a way of enhancing democracy, thwarting vested interests and overcoming marginalisation. This apparent approval of pressure group politics can be contrasted with the low level of public confidence currently enjoyed by elected politicians: one TD, who owed her election in an affluent Dublin constituency largely to her profile as a leading campaigner on women's issues, spoke somewhat plaintively of her surprise at the 'lack of respect once you become a TD', in contrast to that which she commanded when involved in pressure group politics as chairperson of the Women's Political Association and afterwards of the state's Council for the Status of Women.[23]

PRESSURE GROUPS AND INDIVIDUAL PARLIAMENTARIANS

In examining relations between individual parliamentarians and pressure groups of all kinds, it is crucial to note that the imperative of party discipline has always been a formidable counterweight to the leverage which even the most highly organised national or local interests can bring to bear on individual TDs and senators (although, as already noted, some interests also lobby the political parties directly). Discipline is enforced particularly strongly in the two largest parties, and in the Dail the general presumption remains, as it has been for 70 years, that the benefits accruing to a TD from defying the party whip on an issue are usually outweighed by the long term costs.[24] These may include, as well as the indefinite loss of the various benefits of parliamentary party membership and administrative support, long term problems in securing advancement, either within the party or in government. A TD's chances of securing nomination by the party to run at the next election may also be jeopardised. Furthermore, as all TDs feel the tug of their constituents, parliamentary party members who toe the party line and take the local flak are generally unsympathetic to a colleague who, when a constituency issue conflicts with the party line, suddenly discovers his conscience and takes a stand, or worse still attempts to hold the leadership to ransom by intimating that he may have to act unless certain concessions are forthcoming. Perhaps more than in most parliaments, the rules of the Oireachtas game are such that 'personal instrumentality' still largely equates with compliance with the party's wishes.[25] As Michael Gallagher puts it:

> deputies behave not as individuals but as members of a party. When it comes to the crunch, deputies in most parliaments follow the party line; when political life is dominated by political parties ... deputies' orientation to party is stronger than their orientation to parliament ... the solidarity of party voting in the Dail is extraordinarily high, to the extent that any government TD voting against any government bill, apart from those very rare occasions when a free vote is allowed, is likely to be expelled from the parliamentary party.[26]

Party discipline also applies to senators, although in their chamber the rules of the game vary depending on the means by which different senators are elected. The Seanad, consequently, is discussed separately below.

Aspects of the Irish political system, particularly its small scale and the electoral system – PR-STV in multi-seat constituencies – have fostered a form of 'localism' that has played a major role in determining the relationship between individual TDs and the wide range of pressure groups who lobby them. PR-STV places the emphasis more on individual candidates than on political parties and their policies. It therefore produces a high degree of competition at constituency level between candidates from the same political party. TDs consequently spend a great deal of time cultivating a personal vote. Research in this area has generally concentrated on the relationship between TDs and individual constituents, and the much criticised 'brokerage' role of public representatives in dealing with central and local government on such constituents' behalf.[27] The impact of local pressure groups on TDs' workloads has been relatively under-researched, but the electoral system undoubtedly makes both TDs and aspiring candidates particularly vulnerable to them. The preoccupation of TDs with local issues is reinforced by the fact that so many of them came to prominence through local authority service and continue to occupy council seats: of the TDs elected in 1992, '73% were on a local authority [immediately] before entering the Dail, and 90% had been on a local authority at some stage'.[28] During the 1990s there 'has been an increase in grass-roots organisations that are very disenchanted with both politicians and civil servants and, finding the formal structures of the state unsatisfactory, are instead turning towards informal or ad hoc self-help groups'.[29] Such bodies, whether quasi-representative associations such as residents' groups, campaigns on a purely local issue, or the local branches of a national organisation, are becoming one of the two main forms of constituency pressure faced by TDs.

Evidence of the growing significance of local pressure groups at constituency level emerges from the published proceedings of the Dail. By way of illustration, the 551 Dail questions tabled for written answer in the month of May 1997 were reviewed to provide a snapshot of TDs' preoccupations in the weeks running up to the June general election. As the literature would predict, this showed that almost half related to constituency issues rather than to national affairs or policy matters. More surprisingly, however, fully half of the constituency questions clearly reflected the concerns of local pressure groups rather than those of individual constituents. A number related to the efforts of social pressure groups to gain access to policy forums and/or state funding, while others were clearly inspired by the growing 'equal parenting' lobby which has arisen following reform of the laws on marriage breakdown.[30] It seems reasonable to predict that, as pressure group politics mushroom, so TDs will have to spend ever more of their time in propiating these powerful if sometimes transient local forces. In this connection, the experience of Niamh Breathnach, the minister for education from 1992 to 1997, is instructive. After topping her constituency poll in the 1992 election, she ignominiously lost her seat in June 1997 despite having been responsible for reforms in third-level education which should have had particular appeal in her middle class constituency. She attributed the catastrophic decline in her popularity (far in excess of the fall in the Labour Party vote nationally) largely to the actions of local pressure groups, in particular a community group campaigning on the issue of traffic regulation (the business of the local authority, not of central government) and a cystic fibrosis support group lobbying for a new treatment unit in the local hospital. Both of these groups claimed that she had been unhelpful, and these charges against her were diligently aired by her rivals during the campaign.[31]

The perils of incurring the enmity of local pressure groups, both for the conventional political parties and for sitting TDs, is brought home by the impact in recent general elections of essentially single issue candidates. In the 1997 general election two TDs were elected on what were in essence pressure group platforms – one on the bizarre issue of how best to provide an inexpensive multi-channel television relay service in a moutainous region, the other on an anti-water charges ticket.[32] In the two previous elections, a pressure group candidate won a crucial seat in Roscommon as part of a campaign to prevent the closure of a local hospital (1989 and 1992). Often the act simply of threatening to contest an election is sufficient for a local pressure group to extract some concessions from the government via their sitting TDs; sometimes the message is put across through actually fielding candidates. As part of a very successful campaign for improvement in the pay and conditions of members of the defence forces in the 1989 election, 'army wives' candidates supported by the National Army Spouses's Association drew crucial votes away from the established parties in a handful of constituencies with strong army links. This undoubtedly contributed to a policy U-turn by the incoming administration, resulting not only in a pay review and a new accommodation programme but in official recognition of representative bodies for both officers and enlisted men.[33] The 'army wives' provide an interesting and unusual example of the successful exploitation of local factors for a national or sectoral cause. The dismal 1997 general election performance of umbrella parties embracing Catholic/family values/anti-abortion groups demonstrate how difficult it generally is for pressure groups with a national focus or cause to threaten the electoral interests of TDs.

The Seanad requires separate consideration. Its very powerlessness means that party discipline is noticeably slacker. Furthermore, its variegated composition means that in general different kinds of senators have different priorities: the 43 who are elected by a combination of sitting TDs, outgoing senators and members of county councils tend to be party politicians, whether playing the elder statesman on their way out of national politics, trying to make a name in order to get a chance to run for a Dail seat, or marking time in the interval between losing a Dail seat and attempting to regain it at the next election. While the Seanad does not lend itself to the public exercise of brokerage in the way the Dail does – senators cannot table parliamentary questions – it provides status and at least a subordinate place in the legislature. A further 11 senators are nominated after the Dail and Seanad elections by the serving taoiseach (this is to provide a built-in majority for the government of the day, a mechanism which failed in December 1994 when there was a change of government without an intervening general election, obliging the new administration to court Seanad independents assiduously). Nominated members are a mixture of would-be TDs and non-party figures (including some associated with particular good causes), who by convention do not make life difficult for the taoiseach who installed them. The remaining six senators are elected by graduates of the state's two oldest universities, in Irish terms unusually liberal and pluralist constituencies. Consequently, in contrast to most members of the Oireachtas, these university senators have a licence to speak up for minorities and to raise uncomfortable issues: the case for the revision of Ireland's antediluvian laws on contraception, on homosexuality and on various aspects of women's rights, together with other social issues, was first made in the Oireachtas by university senators at a time when TDs of all parties ran scared of raising such indelicacies. In recent years foreign policy questions, human rights problems and development issues have also frequently been aired. University senators are, consequently, good targets for some groups seeking Oireachtas ventilation of their causes. In a more self-interested vein, the university senators exploited their pivotal position in the senate brilliantly during the tortuous passage in 1996 and 1997 of the Universities Act, the first attempt by an Irish government to bring all universities under a single legislative umbrella. Between its initial tabling and its final passage, the bill was amended almost beyond recognition in a direction favourable to the independence of universities from central government control.[34]

PARLIAMENTARIANS, PARTIES AND CORRUPTION

A dark side of relations between pressure groups and the Oireachtas, which particularly affects government TDs, is the issue of the receipt by political parties of financial support from business interests. The Oireachtas has been very slow to admit the possibility that any of its members could be suborned, despite widespread rumours stretching back over many years of the improper exercise of public power by politicians serving unavowed private interests. The political parties were also highly resistant to any suggestion that the identities of donors should ever be disclosed.

A series of scandals have come to light in the last decade involving both state enterprises being prepared for privatisation, and privately owned industries heavily dependent on state patronage. There was also a great deal of controversy about a very curious state-funded purchase of a former teacher training college from a well connected businessman. After particularly strong accusations of political favouritism in the crucial beef export industry, pressure from Fianna Fail's coalition partners forced the establishment of a judicial inquiry in 1991. This marathon exercise had an unsatisfactory outcome: although ample evidence was adduced of systematic tax and export relief fraud, and of political favouritism on a grand scale, in its conclusions the report stopped short of adducing any link between the highly irregular ministerial decisions and administrative practices which it uncovered and the relationships between powerful beef industry figures, and both individual politicians and a range of political parties.[35]

The inquiry did, however, make inevitable the overdue passage in 1995 of the Ethics in Public Office Act, which provides for a register of interests and other precautions against corrupt practices. In 1996 came further legislation providing for the state funding of political parties in proportion to their electoral strength, and prescribing a disclosure regime for private or corporate donations to political parties and individual politicians. In parallel with these developments came the rapid rise and dramatic fall of Michael Lowry, a thrusting young Fine Gael politician and a crusader against cronyism in state/business relations at the time of his appointment to the new Bruton cabinet in January 1995, and a discredited figure by the time he resigned from the government in December 1996 after revelations about his secret and incestuous business and personal financial links with the country's largest supermarket chain, Dunnes Stores. Denying that he had done anything improper as a minister in relation to the controversial award of a mobile telephone franchise, he presented a sometimes mawkish and exculpatory statement about his business dealings and tax affairs to the Dail: 'a painful and unpleasant experience but I have chosen to make my position clear.'[36] His case, together with allegations that a former senior minister had received over £1 million from the same source, was the subject of an initial inquiry and then, when that ran into problems of disclosure, of the McCracken tribunal of inquiry. To general surprise, the tribunal proved highly successful in securing information from banks in Ireland and overseas. The tribunal branded Lowry a tax evader, identified two illegal offshore accounts controlled by him, said that he appeared seriously to have breached company law in his business operations, and pointed out that his personal statement of expiation to the Dail had been patently untrue. Having by then topped the poll as an independent in his rural constituency in the June 1997 election, all this produced from Lowry was another red faced statement: 'I categorically assure this House that it was not my intention to mislead.'[37] The former taoiseach Mr Haughey, whose gilded lifestyle, imperious mien and autocratic manner had long been the object of comment and rumour, at first denied to the tribunal that he had received any financial support from Dunnes Stores.[38] He was later constrained by hard evidence to acknowledge receipt of over £1 million over a four year period while taoiseach between 1987 and 1991. He continued to deny, however, that any consideration was sought or given in return for this munificence. It also emerged that for almost 30 years his financial and tax affairs had been handled and his household expenses paid by a close friend and practising accountant and businessman. Furthermore, it transpired that this man had periodically passed the hat around in business circles on Mr Haughey's behalf, that he controlled the 'Ansbacher accounts' illegally held in a Cayman Islands bank, of which Mr Haughey was one beneficiary, totalling almost £40 million, and that a firm controlled by one of Mr Haughey's sons had also benefited from funds in these accounts. It was 'quite unbelievable' that Haughey would not have known of these illegal off-shore arrangements and the consequent tax evasion, and much of his evidence was 'unacceptable and untrue'. As the tribunal observed, it was 'quite unacceptable' that a taoiseach 'should be supported in his personal lifestyle by gifts' made in secret to him.[39]

The tribunal's revelations were astonishing for the extent of covert payments to Mr Haughey which they disclosed over a four year period. This begged obvious questions about his sources of income during the earlier parts of his lengthy political service. The Oireachtas accordingly established a further tribunal to probe the question of whether business interests might have secured favourable policy decisions by dint of other contributions to either Mr Lowry or Mr Haughey during their ministerial careers. The two major parties mysteriously agreed, however, that it would be improper to determine who else held money in the secret 'Ansbacher accounts', despite the fact that these were plainly illegal and suggested tax evasion on a grand scale. As the journalist who broke the Lowry story put it, 'senior members of ... the country's two largest political parties ... had flagrantly flouted the law. After the biggest political scandal in a generation, the government and the largest opposition party have drawn a line in the Caribbean sand'.[40]

A further shock came in the autumn of 1997 with the resignation from the government and Dail of the powerful minister for foreign affairs, Ray Burke. He had been unable to shake off allegations about his involvement in controversy in his area of north County Dublin, where holders of agricultural land could make vast profits if it could be re-zoned for house building. He argued that there was nothing sinister in a donation of £30,000 in cash made to him at his home in 1989 by an employee of a company with construction interests, whom he had never previously met, who was brought to his house by a prominent builder and party supporter: 'At no time during our meeting were any favours sought or given.' Burke subsequently passed on £10,000 to party headquarters.[41] What was at issue was not Burke's conduct as a minister, but his role when a member of the local authority which carried out controversial re-zonings against professional advice at various times during the 1980s and early 1990s.[42] On the day of his resignation, the Oireachtas established a further tribunal to look into some of the more contentious re-zoning decisions.[43]

This accumulation of evidence of financial impropriety over the last decade, in former taoiseach Haughey's case on an Olympian scale, begs major questions about general standards of probity in Irish public life. The various disclosures also indicate that four of the state's biggest political parties have been heavily dependent on donations from business interests (the radical Democratic Left party is the only significant exception, although the Workers Party from which it split in 1992 was allegedly the beneficiary of funding both from para-military crime and from the Soviet Union).[44] It remains to be seen whether the recently introduced ethics and funding measures will have a permanent impact, or whether further tribunals will in future be required to sluice out the Augean stables of Irish political life.

CONCLUSION

Pressure group politics have become an increasingly important element in national affairs, and the Oireachtas and its members are inevitable targets for groups or interests seeking to influence public policy. TDs whose brokerage work traditionally focused on individual constituents now also have to propiate a growing number of local pressure groups. At national level, pressure groups have become increasingly important to the Oireachtas, not simply for the demands which they make but for the ideas and material which they can provide. The inadequacies of the Oireachtas's own research infrastructure have at times seen some pressure groups acquire undue influence over the deliberations of committees. When it comes to actual parliamentary votes, however, party discipline remains remarkably strong.

It has taken many years for the Oireachtas to face up to some of the more distasteful possibilities which arise when interests attempt to secure favourable consideration from the political system, including at an extreme the bribery of individual politicians. The belated Ethics in Office Act and the Electoral Act at least provide an unequivocal framework, so that politicians and parties in receipt of covert money can no longer plead ignorance or confusion. As the McCracken tribunal concluded, however, 'it may be that the measures ... do not go far enough, as politicians devious enough to deceive the Revenue Commissioners and the public will almost certainly go to equal lengths to deceive the Oireachtas'.[45] When it comes to influence, silent money may still talk.

NOTES

1. E. O'Halpin, 'Partnership Programme Managers in the Reynolds/Spring Coalition, 1993–4: An Assessment', *Irish Political Studies*, 7 (1997), pp.78–90.
2. M. Gallagher, 'The Election of the 27th Dail', in M. Gallagher and M. Laver (eds.), *How Ireland Voted 1992* (Dublin: PSAI Press/Folens, 1993), p.59. R. Sinnott, *Irish Voters Decide: Voting Behaviour in Elections and Referendums since 1918* (Manchester: Manchester University Press, 1994), p.313, gives turnout figures to 1992 as follows: 76.3% (1977), 76.2% (1981), 73.8% (Feb. 1982), 72.9% (Nov. 1982), 73.3% (1987), 68.5% (1989), and 68.5% (1992). The 1997 figure was 66.8%.
3. J. Horgan, *Sean Lemass: The Enigmatic Patriot* (Dublin: Gill & Macmillan, 1997), pp.289–90, 322–5; J. Coakley, 'Society and Political Culture', in J. Coakley and M. Gallagher (eds.), *Politics in the Republic of Ireland*, 2nd edn. (Dublin: PSAI Press/Folens, 1993), pp.40–41; *The Irish Times*, 12 Nov. 1997.
4. B. Kennelly and E. Ward, 'The Abortion Referendums', in Gallagher and Laver, *How Ireland Voted 1992*, pp.122–3.
5. For a racy account of the Lowry and Haughey sagas by the journalist who broke the stories, see S. Smyth, *Thanks a Million, Big Fella* (Dublin: Blackwater Press, 1997).
6. See Horgan, *Lemass*, pp.228–49, and G. Murphy, 'Towards a Corporate State? Sean Lemass and the Realignment of Interest Groups in the Policy Process, 1948–1964', *Dublin City University Business School Research Papers*, No.23 (1996–97), pp.11–13, on the evolution of a consensual approach to national economic policy formulation.
7. As an illustration see the *Second Commission on the Status of Women: Report to Government* (Dublin: Stationery Office, 1993), pp.224–5.
8. *Strategy into the 21st century* (Dublin: National Economic and Social Council, 1996); *Partnership 2000 for Inclusion, Employment and Competitiveness* (Dublin: Government Publications, 1996); *The Irish Times*, 24 Oct. and 19 Dec. 1996.
9. On the reorientation of the Irish public service towards its 'customers', see D. McKevitt and J.F. Keogan, 'Making Sense of Strategy Statements: A User's Guide', *Administration*, Vol.45, No.3 (Autumn 1997), pp.3–6.
10. *Report of the Commission on the Status of Women* (Dublin: Stationery Office, 1973); *Second Commission on the Status of Women*.
11. G. Hussey's diary, 14 Aug. 1983, quoted in her *At the Cutting Edge: Cabinet Diaries, 1982–1987* (Dublin: Gill and Macmillan, 1990), p.53; G. FitzGerald, *All in a Life: An Autobiography* (Dublin: Gill and Macmillan, 1991), pp.416–17, 443–6.
12. Kennelly and Ward, 'The Abortion Referendums', pp.115–16.
13. FitzGerald, *All in a Life*, pp.626–31; Hussey diary, 22 June 1986, in *At the Cutting Edge*, p.222.
14. *The Irish Times*, 27 Nov. 1995.
15. M. Gallagher, 'Parliament', in Coakley and Gallagher (eds.), *Politics in the Republic of Ireland*, pp.137–8.
16. Interview with Ronan O'Brien, Research Officer, the Labour Party, 30 June 1997.

17. See the report by M. O'Connell and T. Harding, *Sunday Business Post*, 29 Sept. 1996.
18. Gallagher, 'Parliament', pp.138–40, 146.
19. Writing in *The Times*, 1 Jan. 1998.
20. Confidential information. The committee published no fewer than 68 reports during its four years' existence.
21. Interview with Monica Barnes, who when a TD was a member of the committee, 1997.
22. E. O'Halpin, 'Irish Parliamentary Culture and the European Union: Formalities to be Observed', in P. Norton (ed.), *National Parliaments and the European Union* (London and Portland, OR: Frank Cass, 1996), pp.132–3; Professor P. Keatinge (Trinity College) and J. Doyle (Dublin City University), speaking at a conference on 'Small States and European Security', Royal Irish Academy, 21 Nov. 1997.
23. Quoted in *The Irish Times*, 7 Dec. 1996.
24. E. O'Halpin, 'Parliamentary Discipline and Tactics in the Fianna Fail Records, 1926–1932', *Irish Historical Studies xxx*, No.120 (Nov. 1997), pp.581–90.
25. On this concept see K. Strom, 'Rules, Reasons and Routines: Legislative Roles in Parliamentary Democracies', *Journal of Legislative Studies*, Vol.3, No.1 (Spring 1997), pp.155–74.
26. Gallagher, 'Parliament', p.146.
27. M. Gallagher and L. Komito, 'Dail Deputies and their Constituency Work', in Coakley and Gallagher (eds.), *Politics in the Republic of Ireland*, pp.151–5.
28. M. Gallagher and L. Komito, 'Dail Deputies', p.150. Note that all ministers, accounting for approximately 20 per cent of TDs, are disbarred from local authority membership
29. Gallagher and Komito, 'Dail Deputies', p.165.
30. *Dail Debates*, Vol.478, 7 May, and Vol.479, 8, 13 and 14 May 1997.
31. Interview with Niamh Breathnach, 1 July 1997.
32. These are Thomas Gildea and Joe Higgins. Mr Higgins, a one-time member of Militant, has a wider agenda as founder of the Socialist Party.
33. *Report of the Commission on the Remuneration and Conditions of Service in the Defence Forces* (Dublin: Stationery Office, 1990), p.xiv.
34. Conversations with Dr John Horgan, at various times until 1989 a university senator, TD, and MEP, and with a serving university senator, both 1997.
35. *Report of the Tribunal of Inquiry into the Beef Processing Industry* (Dublin: Government Publications, 1994); Fintan O'Toole, *Meanwhile back at the Ranch: The Politics of Irish Beef* (London: Vintage, 1995).
36. *Dail Debates*, Vol.473, cols.698–9, 19 Dec. 1996.
37. *Dail Debates*, Vol.480, col.616, 15 Sept. 1997.
38. For earlier explorations of Mr Haughey, see J. Joyce and P. Murtagh, *The Boss: Charles J. Haughey in Government* (Dublin: Poolbeg, 1983), and B. Arnold, *Haughey: His Life and Unlucky Deeds* (London: Viking, 1993).
39. McCracken Report, pp.52, 72–3.
40. Smyth, 'Thanks a Million', p.172.
41. *Dail Debates*, Vol.480, cols.617–18, 15 Sept. 1997.
42. *The Irish Times*, 8 Aug. 1997.
43. *Dail Debates*, Vol.481, cols.51–103, 7 Oct. 1997.
44. High Court testimony of Chief Superintendent Egan, as reported in *The Sunday Tribune*, 24 Aug. 1997. See also reports from the second de Rossa libel trial in *The Irish Times*, 1, 5 and 8 March 1997. J.F. Burke, 'Recently Released Material on Soviet Intelligence Operations', *Intelligence and National Security*, Vol.8, No.2 (April 1993), p.248.
45. McCracken Report, p.75.

CHAPTER 8

The European Parliament: Getting the House in Order

MARK P. SHEPHARD

Analysing pressure group activity at the European level is a complex process. Not only are there multiple European institutions to be considered, but changes in the powers of these institutions over time has precipitated changes in how pressure groups and institutions go about their activities. Until the Single European Act (SEA), group activities at the European level mainly involved lobbying at the initiation and formulation stages (primarily the Commission) and at the deliberation stage (primarily the Council of Ministers). Since the SEA, lobbying of European Union (EU) institutions has become more diversified and complex. In the case of the European Parliament (EP), a gradual increase in powers since the SEA has resulted in lobbyists approaching MEPs 'like bees in a honey pot'.[1] This chapter addresses the changing position of the EP in relation to pressure groups. It considers how the Parliament's improved capacity for affecting outcomes has made it more of a target for lobbying and it considers how the EP is used as a channel for publicity and interest articulation. Finally, it considers the consequences of pressure group activities for the EP and the reaction of the EU institutions to increased lobbying.

THE CHANGING POSITION OF THE EP IN RELATION
TO PRESSURE GROUPS

The EP is an interesting anomaly to the first hypothesis posited in the introduction that parliaments have been pushed from the initiating and formulating stages of the policy process, leaving them operating instead primarily at the deliberative stage. The case of the EP shows that over time the Parliament has grown in effectiveness at all stages. However, the EP fits the hypothesis to the extent that most of the influence of the Parliament today centres around the capacity to affect outcomes at the deliberative stage.

The EP is very much a legislature in flux. Less than 50 years old, the institution has experienced multiple improvements to its legislative powers over time. Most notable advances in powers have been secured since the SEA of 1986. The co-operation procedure of the SEA, for example, gave the EP the opportunity for a second reading and the right to reject legislation, albeit conditional upon an absolute majority in the plenary and lack of consensus in the Council. Subsequent advances have been achieved through the 1993 Maastricht and 1997 Amsterdam treaties, which respectively introduced and extended policy areas considered under the co-decision procedure. The co-decision procedure gives the Parliament outright powers of rejection and the chance to bargain directly with the Council. However, these powers have not been distributed evenly across policy areas. Powers now range from the more common and yet least influential right to consultation on legislation, to the less common and yet more influential right to co-decision with the Council of Ministers.[2]

Consequently, the capacity of the Parliament to affect outcomes tends to depend on the policy area and associated procedure that each piece of legislation is considered under. For instance, legislation in areas such as foreign and security policy is considered under the usually least influential procedure of consultation. While consultation permits the Parliament to amend, adopt or reject a piece of legislation, the final decision is determined by the Council. Meanwhile, legislation in areas such as education or public health are considered under the usually more influential procedure of co-decision. In terms of the quantity of legislation, the number of measures considered by the EP under the consultation procedure from 1987 to 1996 was 1,717. The totals for the co-operation and co-decision procedures were 455 and 92 respectively.[3] Controlling for the fact that the co-decision procedure was only introduced in 1993, the Commission figures for 1996 show that 164 measures were considered under consultation, compared with 31 measures for the first reading of the co-operation procedure and 34 measures for the first reading of the co-decision procedure. Of these, amendments were proposed in 89 of the 164 consultations, 26 of the 31 co-operations, and 25 of the 34 co-decisions.[4] While quantity tells us nothing about the quality of the legislation, it is clear that although the deliberative powers available to the Parliament have improved considerably over time, most of the measures that pass through the EP still have to be considered under the usually less influential procedure of consultation.

Nevertheless, since the SEA the EP has become a target for increasing pressure group activity. Several explanations can be posited. First, and most obviously, the Parliament's capacity to affect outcomes has increased substantially for those policy areas that are now considered using the co-operation and co-decision procedures. Between 1993 and 1995, for example, the EP successfully rejected two pieces of legislation under co-operation and two under co-decision. In addition to these procedures, the Parliament also has powers to determine association and accession agreements with third parties. Over the years, several association agreements have been affected, for example, the withholding of consent on protocols with Israel in 1988, Morocco in 1992 and Syria in 1992 and 1993. Furthermore, the EP has been successful in helping to initiate legislative projects. The most notable of these was the 1984 parliamentary initiative for a new treaty which paved the way for the Council's adoption of the SEA. Further initiatives detailing treaty revisions have been influential in decision making concerning the Maastricht and Amsterdam Treaties.

Second, many pressure groups have come to realise that the EP has much potential as a powerful institution because of its independence from the Commission and Council. Unlike the House of Commons, for example, confidence in the EP is not conditional upon majority support of key components of the government's legislative programme. Instead, the EP is responsible primarily to its electorate. In addition, while the Commission and Council have no powers of censure on the activities of the Parliament, the EP has a formalised vote of confidence on the choice of the Commission President and Commission, as well as powers of censure. Consequently, the EP has greater latitude than many national legislatures when amending or rejecting Commission and Council decisions. Realistically, however, the Parliament is conscious of the need to secure a sound working relationship with the Commission and Council. In turn, how far it exercises its authority will depend in part on the political climate of the relationship it has established with the Commission and Council.

Third, while limitations of procedures such as consultation may reduce the overall capacity of the Parliament to affect outcomes, increasing numbers of lobbyists are beginning to recognise that the procedural powers of the Parliament are not static. As procedural powers are up-graded, and the areas to which they apply are steadily broadened, pressure groups which realistically expect little influence from the Parliament today are nonetheless building relationships so that they can better influence the Parliament when it has a greater capacity to determine outcomes.

Fourth, pressure groups have other interests besides influencing legislation. Whether or not the Parliament can affect outcomes, it can provide a legitimate forum and channel for the publicising of issues. In accepting a campaign, MEPs can attract media attention and help raise public awareness and pressure for resolution of issues. In the case of the EP, multiple examples exist of the power of the Parliament to help raise awareness and influence in relation to pressure group campaigns. One of the fields in which the EP has been most active is in raising awareness of human rights issues around the world. Recent examples include resolutions on banning land mines, efforts to secure solutions to human rights abuses in Turkey, and moves to link agreements with non-EU countries to the provision of basic levels of social protection for employees.[5] Further media attention is created for those recipients of the Parliament's much publicised Sakharov prize for freedom of thought. Past recipients who have benefited from the publicity surrounding the prize have included Aung San Suu Kyi and Nelson Mandela. Other examples of publicity include the attention given to the promotion of animal welfare issues as well as issues affecting groups from motorbike enthusiasts to pensioners and the disabled. In many cases, causes publicised by the EP have been successful in influencing the decision-making process. Examples include legislation to ban the import of baby seal products and amendments to legislation easing restrictions on motorbikes.

Fifth, the Parliament provides multiple forums and opportunities for pressure groups to articulate interests. Common forums include parliamentary committees and hearings, inter-groups, conferences and question times.

There are approximately 20 committees and several sub-committees that operate in the Parliament. These committees broadly correspond to the departments or Directorates General of the Commission and include committees on Budgets, Transport and Tourism, and Environment, Public Health and Consumer Protection.[6] The extent of lobbying activity largely depends on the activism and the breadth and depth of the spheres of competence of each committee. One of the most heavily lobbied committees in the Parliament is the Committee on Environment, Public Health and Consumer Protection.

Committees prepare discussion papers and reports that direct the Parliament through the various details and consequences of proposed legislation. Consequently, they are natural targets for pressure groups seeking to influence the decisions of the Parliament. Key targets within the committee are the chair and rapporteur. Contact with the chair is important, as the chair sets the legislative agenda and gives advice to the Parliament on what positions to take. Meanwhile, groups are keen to lobby the rapporteur as it is the rapporteur's responsibility to prepare a report on the Parliament's position in relation to proposed legislation. While not all pressure groups may be consulted, many rapporteurs work hard to consult as many differently affected groups as they can. Often it is in the best interest of the parliamentarian to engage in consultations with pressure groups as this serves a dual purpose of more complete information on which to base a report, as well as greater publicity for the goals of the report and the MEP. In the case of a 1996 report on the rights of disabled people by Mary Banotti of the Committee of Petitions, for example, the report and the position of the rapporteur were strengthened by the extensive consultations that had occurred. In drafting the report, Banotti had contacted all MEPs and European and national disability non-governmental organisations in the European Disability Forum.[7]

Other committee forums include hearings. These are conducted by committees interested in gaining expertise and evidence from third parties. Information is typically used to help committees draft reports. Recent examples include hearings on the competitiveness of European industry, the EU and space, the financial consequences of enlargement, protecting the European taxpayer, free speech and media rights, and the Community Transit System. In the case of the last of these, representatives of Rothmans and the European Confederation of Tobacco Retailers were invited to give evidence on how loopholes in the Community Transit System were affecting their abilities to compete with those organisations evading the rules.[8] Evidence from groups assists the Parliament in the creation or amendment of legislative proposals which are sometimes influential in subsequent legislation, for example, the tightening of regulations for Common Agricultural Policy refunds.[9]

Since 1979, a growing area of contact between MEPs and pressure groups has been through the forum of inter-groups. Inter-groups are cross-party, cross-nationality groups that are brought together by a common interest. Current estimates of the number of inter-groups operating in the EP put the total at around 50 and include groups on a myriad of interests from aging to consumer affairs and sports, and tourism. In the case of the sports inter-group, objectives primarily entail furthering the involvement of the European Union in sporting matters. Membership is open to any MEP and meetings are attended by a diversity of outside groups including representatives of many governmental and non-governmental sports organisations, as well as representatives from the Commission. Inter-groups are mostly unofficial and operate in less formal environments than committees and hearings. Consequently, they often provide an opportunity for all manner of interests to voice their concerns. In turn, inter-groups offer an alternative forum for pressure groups to establish relationships that might be more difficult to achieve in more formal circumstances. Inter-groups frequently meet during the plenary sessions and are active in utilising as many procedural means as they can to further their goals. In the case of the sports inter-group, recent activity has included oral questions to the Commission, pressure for extending treaty provisions to sport, as well as influence in establishing committee reports.[10]

Further articulation of interests occurs during parliamentary conferences and exhibitions. Conferences are sponsored by the Parliament or its committees and have included a range of issues from security and co-operation in Europe to world food, energy, the environment and regional policy. One of the most recent conferences considered economic and social cohesion and the contribution of local authorities to a more democratic union. The conference occurred in October 1996 and was sponsored by the EP, the Committee on Regional Policy and the Committee of the Regions. The conference attracted approximately 180 elected representatives of EU local authorities, more than 120 MEPs, and observers from the Council, Commission and national parliaments.[11] The outcome of the conference was a detailed declaration listing over 30 recommendations for action at the Intergovernmental Conference (IGC). Recommendations included that the IGC broaden the EP's co-decision procedure to include regulations governing the structural funds and the cohesion fund. Although this recommendation was not implemented, the consideration of structural and cohesion funds was up-graded to the assent procedure. Other tactics for pressure groups include participation in exhibitions usually held during the plenary session. Several exhibitions attracting multiple groups are typically on display each month the Parliament is sitting. Displays offer a means for attracting media attention and give pressure groups opportunities for the articulation of interests to MEPs.

Finally, interests can be articulated through parliamentary questions put to the Commission and the Council. Commission statistics for 1996 show that the Parliament addressed 5,445 questions to the Commission and Council (4,131 written, 261 oral with debate, and 1,053 during question time).[12] While not all of these questions were motivated by consultations with pressure groups, many questions are addressed based on the information that groups provide. The sports inter-group, for example, has been instrumental in persuading MEPs to table questions on the controversial Bosman judgment.[13] More recent examples include questions championing the cause of a range of groups from small banana producers to road haulage companies.[14] The response of the Commission and Council tends to depend on the issue and its salience to the existing operations of the EU. Nevertheless, the replies of the Commission and Council do suggest that in many cases questioning by the Parliament is an effective forum for the articulation of interests and influence of legislation.

THE RISE OF PRESSURE GROUP ACTIVITIES IN RELATION TO THE EP

Although no precise indicators exist for measuring the extent of pressure group activities undertaken in relation to the EP, a number of measures can be used to illustrate the substantial growth in activities. First, various estimates exist as to the growth and number of lobbyists. Andersen and Eliassen, for example, estimate that the number of lobbying organisations in the EU rose from approximately 700 in 1986 to 3,000 by 1990. Meanwhile, the total number of individual lobbyists was reported to have increased from approximately 6,000 in 1986 to 10,000 by 1990.[15] Another report in the January 1996 edition of *EP News* also identified the figure of 10,000 individual lobbyists. Profiles of the lobbying groups in Brussels suggest that they include approximately 140 professional public affairs consultancies, 160 law firms, more than 500 trade associations and over 200 major multinational corporations. In addition, other lobbying groups include multiple diplomats and around 60 local and regional authorities of the Member States.[16]

Second, research shows that contact between MEPs and pressure groups is increasing. A 1996 survey of British MEPs (see Table 8.1) showed that 96 per cent felt that the mailbag had increased since they were first elected. On average, British MEPs reported that they now received 81 pieces of mail per week from businesses and pressure groups. Of this, 41 per cent comprised circulars, 25 per cent requested meetings with MEPs, and 17 per cent were invitations to receptions or dinners.[17] On average, British MEPs accepted 55 per cent of invitations to meetings and 19 per cent of those to receptions or dinners, and met with a number of selected constituency groups per month. In terms of contact with selected constituency groups such as farmers and trade unions, MEPs averaged four talks per month.

Third, evidence for increased pressure group activity can be detected from the statistics on the number of people visiting the EP. Between 1994 and 1997, the number of visitors to EP sessions in Brussels increased more than threefold, from 4,685 to 15,950. Meanwhile, visits at other times rose from 34,279 to 51,900 over the same period.[18] Although not all of these visits can be attributed to members of pressure groups, earlier analyses of

THE EUROPEAN PARLIAMENT

TABLE 8.1
CONTACT BETWEEN BRITISH MEPs AND BUSINESSES
AND PRESSURE GROUPS

Quantity of mail received each week from businesses and pressure groups
81 pieces*
Proportion comprising circulars	41%
Proportion comprising requests for meetings/appointments	25%
Proportion comprising requests to attend receptions/dinners	17%
Other	17%
Total	100%
Proportion of meetings/appointments accepted	55%
Proportion of receptions/dinners accepted	19%
Proportion agreeing the mailbag has grown since they were first elected	96%

Proportion mailbag has grown for those first elected in:
a) 1979	75% (N=3)
b) 1984	63% (N=4)
c) 1989	70% (N=6)
d) 1994	53% (N=6)
e) **Average**	65% (N=19)

Average number of talks to selected constituency groups (e.g. Farmers, trade unions) per month	4
Average number of visits and inspections (e.g. Schools, businesses) in the constituency per month	4.4

Notes: *N=24.

Results are drawn from a September 1996 survey of 26 out of 87 UK MEPs. Surveys were distributed to all UK MEPs and were returned by 29% of Labour MEPs (N=18), 28% of Conservative MEPs (N=5), 100% of Liberal Democrats (N=2), and 50% of Scottish Nationalists (N=1). The sample is broadly representative of those elected in each election.

visitors estimated that approximately 75 per cent of passes issued during sessions were for lobbyists.[19] Other forms of contact exist but are harder to measure. These include informal contacts and communications via telephone, e-mail and fax.

In all, the case of the EP supports the second hypothesis that parliaments are a target and a channel for group pressure. The EP not only has a growing capacity to affect outcomes (reflected in the growth of pressure group activities), but has also become a more important channel for publicity and the articulation of interests. Indeed, during the 1990s scholars started to rank the Parliament ahead of the Council in terms of the interest it received from the activities of pressure groups.[20] The increased pressures that this interest has placed on the Parliament has led to a series of institutional attempts at restoring balance between the needs of all parties.

CONSEQUENCES FOR THE EP AND REACTIONS TO IMBALANCE

Attempts at establishing stricter rules and codes of conduct have taken many years to fulfil. One of the main concerns and obstacles to forms of regulation has been the fear that this would detract from the best interests of the legislative process. In the case of the EP, pressure groups serve several important functions. First, they provide MEPs with invaluable information which can be used in anything from amendments and reports to questions. Without contact from pressure groups, MEPs would lack the information that they require to fulfil their legislative responsibilities. In addition, pressure groups help serve as a channel for EU institutions to interact with each other. Conferences and meetings, for example, often bring parliamentarians and commissioners and ministers together. Again, this may serve as a conduit for improving the legislative process, as it can facilitate contacts and better working relationships between parties.

A second concern for MEPs has been to prevent regulation from impeding the range of opportunities that pressure groups provide. First, MEPs can use their pursuit of interests to publicise the extent of their activities and achievements to the electorate. Depending on the size of the constituency of the MEP and the groups that s/he wants to reach, forms of communication will vary from constituency newsletters to political group and issue-specific newsletters. By virtue of their smaller electoral districts, British MEPs tend to make most use of the constituency newsletter. British newsletters come in a variety of formats, but many offer colour photographs of consultations with groups alongside briefs that depict a range of activities and achievements. Political group and issue-specific newsletters primarily target interested parties from cross-national audiences. *Euro MP*, for example, is a weekly newsletter of the Socialist Group in the Parliament. Mainly aimed at journalists, it contains briefs of forthcoming Socialist Group activities that may be of interest to the media. Without the information and opportunities that pressure groups provide, many of the newsletters would have little worthy of publication. Second, pursuit of interests may also serve career goals within the Parliament. For instance, career opportunities within political groups and committees depend in part on the expertise and contacts that MEPs can accrue from their consultations with third parties. A political group's choice for the prestigious role of rapporteur, for example, often depends on the degree of expertise of the MEP. Third, pursuit of interests is important for those MEPs wishing to further the interests of a 'worthy cause'. Causes and the publicity that they attract range from the much publicised efforts of Roger Barton on behalf of motorcyclists to Claudia Roth's less publicised work on lesbian and gay rights.

While contact between pressure groups and MEPs continues to be of benefit to both parties, problems of imbalance increasingly began to surface as the powers of the Parliament were extended. Tensions quickly heightened in the EP as few mechanisms and resources were in place to deal with these increases in pressure. First, MEPs have witnessed sharp increases in the volume of information being sent by lobbyists. Here the problem arose of information overload. Many MEPs not only started to receive more information than they could process themselves, but more information than their assistants could realistically process either.

Second, relatively limited restrictions on access to the working spaces of the EP meant that MEPs encountered more pressures for direct contact, as well as for space and resources. Once inside the buildings of the EP, lobbyists could have access to MEPs in a variety of settings. Unlike many national parliaments, MEPs could encounter lobbyists at the doors of their offices, and at the exits from the chamber in Strasbourg. In addition, lobbyists made increasing use of other parliamentary spaces, such as the committee rooms, the libraries, and the bars and restaurants. As well as increasing encroachments upon space, MEPs also faced an increase in the competition for resources. In particular, many MEPs began to face a shortage of documentation as lobbyists exhausted parliamentary supplies of materials. Meanwhile, assistants complained of competition for other resources, such as telephones and photocopying machines.

Third, increased lobbyist activities in such an unregulated environment led to the more serious abuse of parliamentary practices. Abuses ranged from gifts for questions to foreign trips in exchange for votes. One of the more serious alleged abuses involved trips to Indonesia in return for voting compliance on the position of the Indonesian government in relation to East Timor.[21] Although the proportion of MEPs and lobbyists engaged in such practices have been small, many within the Parliament have long been keen to establish stricter rules and codes of conduct.

The first attempt at regulation came in May 1991 when the Committee on Rules of Procedure and the Verification of Credentials and Immunities (CPR) appointed the Belgian Socialist MEP Marc Galle to draft a report detailing a code of conduct and a means for registering lobbyists. The recommendations of the report were detailed and offered many solutions to the problems that the EP was facing. First, the report proposed an annual register of lobbyists. Second, the report delineated between areas of access in the Parliament and areas that were 'out of bounds' (such as offices and libraries). Third, a lobbyist code of conduct was proposed with many strict requirements such as rules against the sale of parliamentary documents. Finally, the report recommended a separate annual register of financial interests for MEPs and staff.

However, the report never made it to the vote in the plenary because the CPR failed to resolve a number of issues before the term of the Parliament ended in 1994. One of the most important disputes revolved around the definition of a lobbyist. By restricting his definition to those acting on behalf of a third party, Galle had omitted to include large proportions of lobbyists such as private actors. Another problem with the report was that many of the proposals were so detailed as to be both non-implementable and problematic for the Parliament itself; for instance, preventing lobbyists from later selling parliamentary documents and policing of 'out of bounds' areas. Finally, issues of lobbyist regulation and public conduct did not have the same sense of urgency in the 1989–94 Parliament as they did by the time of the 1994–99 Parliament.

Although the Galle Report faced an insurmountable barrage

of problems, it did stir action on many fronts. The Commission feared that the Parliament's quest for regulation would be inimical to its own interests. The Commission believed that regulation would threaten the free flow of information between European institutions and interests.[22] The importance behind the idea of a free flow of information was that informed policy choices could only be made if access to lobbyists remained as open as possible. Ideas such as registers and access restrictions would only impede exchanges of information. Registers would tend to alienate communications from those groups not listed, while access restrictions would serve to decrease the channels of communication available.

In the wake of the Galle Report, the preferred tactic of the Commission was to promote self-regulation. To this end, the Secretariat of the Commission made repeated calls for lobbyists to draft their own self-regulatory code. Although the response from lobbyists was slow, the Commission organised a series of meetings in which it offered lobbyists' suggestions on possible codes. The broader guidelines of the Commission became known as the 'Ten Commandments'[23] and were eventually incorporated into a self-regulatory code that public-affairs experts applied in relation to their dealings with all EU institutions. The code included requirements to identify name, company and interest represented; accurately represent own status and nature of enquiries and links with EU institutions; honour confidential information and confidentiality requirements of EU institutions; accurately disseminate information; not sell EU documents for profit to third parties; not offer financial inducements to EU officials; and avoid professional conflicts of interest.[24]

While a step in the right direction and endorsed by the EP, the code proved problematic for a number of reasons. First, the code was written and primarily endorsed by public affairs groups. It was not a code that could easily be endorsed by all interest groups, for example, trade associations. Second, the code was viewed by many as weak. Not only did the code require minimal standards of self-regulation, but many of these standards contained loopholes. From the perspective of the EP, one of the main loopholes in the code was that restrictions on financial inducements referred to EU officials and made no specific mention of MEPs and their staff.[25] Although public affairs groups later agreed to an EP amendment that tightened the requirement to include MEPs and their staff, many within the EP remained convinced that self-regulatory codes were not sufficient for the Parliament.

This view gained prominence again early in the 1994–99 Parliament. Following the failure of the Galle report in the 1989–94 Parliament, the CRP requested authorisation to draw up a new report on lobbying in the EP shortly after the 1994 elections. Within three months the report was approved by the President of the Parliament and British Socialist Glyn Ford was appointed as rapporteur by the CRP. At the same time the CRP also requested authorisation to draw up a report on the declaration of members' financial interests in the EP. Similarly approved, French Liberal Jean-Thomas Nordmann was eventually appointed rapporteur by the CRP.[26]

THE FORD AND NORDMANN REPORTS

The initial recommendations of the Ford Report were motivated by a number of concerns. The first concern was to produce a report that would be more acceptable to the EP than the Galle Report. To this end the Ford Report avoided the definitional problems of its predecessor by defining lobbyists in more general terms. Rather than categorising types of lobbyists as Galle had done, Ford referred to lobbyists as 'anyone from outside Parliament who wishes to be allowed to enter on a regular basis to supply information to Members within the framework of their mandate'.[27] Such a broad definition attempted to avoid the inequitable and less tenable situation of having to draw distinctions between groups.

The second concern was motivated by the growing pressure of interest groups and aimed to move beyond the minimalist position of self-regulation that the Commission favoured. As Ford noted in his explanatory statement: 'A set of regulations is certainly needed given the proliferation of enterprises lobbying the European institutions and, more particularly, the European Parliament.'[28] Compounding the emphasis on regulation was the fear that unregulated lobbyist activities could bring the Parliament into disrepute as they had in many of the national legislatures in the EU. In the UK, as reported in Chapter 2, concerns about the conduct of MPs and lobbyists were being raised by the Committee on Standards in Public Life chaired by Lord Nolan. Published several months before the Ford Report, the Nolan Report found that respect for the House of Commons was being eroded by the activities of some MPs and lobbyists. Concerns that the same fate could await the EP are illustrated by Ford's statement that 'The total lack of any supervision of such (lobbyist) activities means that they are being conducted in an almost clandestine manner which is giving rise to rumours of a kind which might discredit Parliament and some of its Members'.[29]

Addressing these concerns, the Ford Report proposed that frequent access to the Parliament be conditional upon two forms of regulation. First, permanent passes (reviewed annually) would be provided to those lobbyists giving the College of Quaestors a formal undertaking to respect a code of conduct. Second, the issue of a permanent pass would also require that lobbyists sign a public register and pay a registration fee to be administered by the College of Quaestors. The public register would detail 'any benefits, subsidies, gifts or services of any nature rendered to Members, officials or assistants, with a value in excess of ECU 1000 per beneficiary per calendar year'.[30] In addition, the Ford Report sought stricter standards for parliamentary assistants. Assistants would be required to register with the College of Quaestors and 'sign a written statement to the effect that they neither represent nor defend any interests other than those connected with their duties'.[31] Combined, Ford argued that this framework would not only set standards for transparency and conduct, but would also permit lobbyists, MEPs and assistants to continue with the important processes of information exchange.

Similar objectives were raised by the Nordmann Report which addressed the other half of the equation, the declaration of MEPs' financial interests. While existing rules required detailed declaration of professional activities and the listing of relevant paid functions or activities, the Nordmann Report sought to make these requirements more explicit. To this end, Nordmann proposed a more accessible public register to be administered by the College of Quaestors. Within the register each MEP would make a personal and detailed declaration of the source and nature of all gifts or benefits over ECU 1,000. In addition, Nordmann proposed that MEPs declare all assets, including 'movable and immovable property, investment funds, shares, bonds, etc.'.[32] Again, all details would be expected to be updated annually.

Combined, both reports took a simple and yet detailed departure from existing codes of conduct. However, some of the detail proved difficult for many MEPs to accept when the reports finally reached the plenary. In the January 1996 EP plenary meeting a majority of MEPs failed to agree to the proposed new rules of procedure. In particular, most disagreements centred around the ECU amount of the gifts to be registered. For instance, MEPs from the European People's Party (EPP) and the Green Group expressed concerns over the minimum threshold of ECU 1,000. The EPP tabled an amendment requiring lobbyists not to provide any gift or payment to an MEP which might possibly influence a vote. Similarly, MEPs of the Green Group argued that the ECU 1,000 threshold was a licence to supply gifts and payments up to that amount. A second Green objection concerned the proposal to limit the associations and activities of parliamentary assistants with lobbyists. Greens argued that it was unfair to burden assistants with obligations while their role and status had yet to be clearly defined.[33] Also, by severing the link between assistants and lobbyists, many MEPs were concerned that they would lose benefits such as expert advice and funded assistant positions. Other concerns were raised about how regulation would interfere with the exchange of information. Ultimately, lack of consensus between the groups led to both reports being sent back to the Committee for further deliberations.

Although the regulation of lobbyists and MEPs' interests had yet to be resolved, a number of advances were achieved. First, the Party of European Socialists (PES) reacted quickly to the plenary defeats. Socialist Leader Pauline Green and Glyn Ford promptly announced that the Socialist Group intended to introduce a detailed register of members' interests and allow members from all political groups to take part.[34] Second, partly because of the EP initiative on the regulatory need to check abuses, the Commission and Council of Ministers made a series of concessions themselves. In the case of the Commission, EP demands for regulatory codes of conduct were realised after MEPs attempted to block commissioner allowances in the wake of a series of allegations concerning payments from outside bodies. One of the more serious allegations involved the 'cash for diaries' scandal that enveloped Commissioner Ritt Bjerregaard.[35] Responding to the EP pressure and the series of allegations against it, the Commission adopted a code of conduct specifying the responsibilities of individual commissioners in relation to their duties and expenses from third parties. The code obliges commissioners not to receive financial remuneration for occupations and engagements with third parties, for instance, writing newspaper columns and lecture tours. However, exceptions are permitted in the publication of books and the receipt of royalties provided the Commission President is informed. The code also calls for all travel expenses to be deducted from the commissioner's budgets.[36] Meanwhile, the Council adopted its own code of conduct that addressed the need for greater transparency in relation to the reporting of Council meetings. Communications with the press are reportedly now more informative than they used to be.[37]

Although the Parliament failed to institute its own system of regulation in the January 1996 plenary, the political climate was right for some form of solution. Combined with the changes that the Council and Commission had implemented, media and public reaction to the failure of the Ford and Nordmann reports prompted the leadership of the Parliament to renew efforts into finding a tenable framework for the oversight of lobbyist and MEP activities. By June 1996, Ford and Nordmann had amended their reports to incorporate some of the concerns that had been raised since their first publication. One of the most notable of the modifications was the decision to soften the position on the reporting of MEP assets. After much deliberation and amending the EP finally agreed to an initial framework for regulation in the July 1996 plenary.

In terms of transparency and members' financial interests, the EP agreed that the Quaestors should keep a register in which each MEP shall make a personal, detailed declaration of (1) professional activities and any other remunerated functions or activities; and (2) any support received by third parties (identity to be disclosed), whether financial or in terms of staff or material except those supplied by the EP. Members also agreed to refrain from accepting any other gift, payment or benefit in the performance of their duties. While no agreement could be reached on the minimum threshold for gift reporting, MEPs did agree to register 'significant' gifts in addition to the requirement that all financial interests be reported before any relevant debate. Finally, as well as agreeing to make the register open to public inspection, members agreed to be subject to the obligations imposed on them by the legislation of the Member State in which they were elected as regards the declaration of assets.[38] In terms of lobbyists, the EP agreed to make the Quaestors responsible for the issuing of passes in return for the respect of a code of conduct and the signing of a public register. Details of the code of conduct were left to be worked out in subsequent reports together with reports on the further control of pressure groups and parliamentary assistants.

In October 1996, Ford was appointed rapporteur for the CRP Report on the code of conduct governing lobbyists. The report was published in March 1997 and proposed tighter access limits for those registered assistants not working exclusively as assistants as well as a code of conduct for lobbyists. The code of conduct proposed that registered lobbyists (1) state the interest or interests they represent with members of the Parliament, their staff or officials of the Parliament; (2) refrain from any action designed to obtain information dishonestly; (3) not claim any formal relationship with the Parliament in any dealings with third parties; (4) not circulate for a profit to third parties copies of documents obtained from the Parliament; (5) refrain from offering gifts or benefits to MEPs; (6) declare any assistance provided in the appropriate register; (7) comply with staff regulations and MEP rules when recruiting former officials; (8) obtain the prior consent of the MEP(s) for employment of assistants and declare that employment in the register; (9) submit a report each year (with a view to securing the extension of their passes) on their activities carried out with the aim of influencing decision making in the Parliament; and (10) lose passes in the case of any breach of the code.[39]

The report reached the plenary in the May 1997 part session and was generally well received. Two main obstacles to passage surfaced and the final code of conduct agreed by the Parliament reflected these. In particular, members from the EPP were concerned that the amendment tightening access for those assistants not working exclusively as assistants should be considered in more detail by the Report on Parliamentary Assistants by Klaus-Heiner Lehne. The second concern focused on the waste of requiring third parties to produce annual reports, for instance, Brendan Donnelly of the EPP argued that this would lead to unnecessary double accounting since MEPs were already required to produce their own annual reports.[40] Consequently, the final code agreed by the Parliament omitted reference to the requirements for assistant access and annual reports from third parties.

Further parliamentary initiative in regulating the activities of lobbyists is expected following the reports of Klaus-Heiner Lehne and Shaun Spiers. Lehne has been appointed rapporteur by the CRP to report on the position of parliamentary assistants, while Spiers has been appointed by the CRP to report on the control of interest groups. Like the code of conduct report, both reports will aim to substantiate further the initial framework documents on lobbying and transparency of members' interests agreed in July 1996. Meanwhile, other initiatives have included hearings on the activities of inter-groups, tightening of rules governing travel expenses, and moves to close salary differentials between MEPs.

The likely implications for the political system of the many reforms are varied. First, concerns have been raised that registration of interests will create a two-tier system in which registered groups will receive higher status and rewards than non-registered groups, for example, privileged meetings and access to documentation and facilities.[41] However, fears that registration will exaggerate the differences between insider and outsider groups have been over-stated. The EP still remains a body relatively open to interests, for example, barriers to the access of documentation have recently been reduced by extending supply to the Internet. Moreover, the new regulations of the Parliament are not intended to keep pressure groups out. They are intended to ensure compliance with basic rules and codes of conduct and set exemplary standards for other institutions in the EU to follow. If the rewards for registered groups do prove to be large, then this will provide an incentive for the non-registered to participate. Indeed, fears of a two-tier system will arguably encourage a high degree of compliance with the Parliament's scheme.

Second, at a time when support for many national parliaments has decreased, the comparatively extensive decisions of the EP to balance regulation of lobbyists with greater transparency of members' interests could prove beneficial in securing higher levels of support from EU citizens. Indeed, getting the House in order before the decline in public support may prove to have been an important strategy for the Parliament as it could help serve the EP in its future quest for an extension of powers.

CONCLUSION

The case of the EP fits the two hypotheses of the volume. First, although the law-making competence of the Parliament has only improved with time, the EP is nonetheless a legislature that operates primarily at the deliberative stage. Second, although eclipsed by the attention the Commission receives, the EP is increasingly a target for group pressure because of its growing consequences for the political system. Consequences are manifest in the growing procedural opportunities for affecting outcomes, as well as the increasing diversity of forums for publicity and articulation of interests. At the same time, pressure group activities have been shown to have important consequences for the work of the Parliament. As well as providing invaluable sources of information for a range of legislative responsibilities, pressure groups are also found to serve a myriad of needs, such as publicity and career development. Meanwhile, the EP has adopted a relatively extensive review of its rules of procedure in order that it may better control imbalance between MEPs and pressure groups. Compared with many national parliaments, the EP has been getting its House in order.

THE EUROPEAN PARLIAMENT

NOTES

1. *European Parliament: The Week*, 15–19 Jan. 1996, p.24.
2. For further information see, M. Shephard, 'The European Parliament: Crawling, Walking and Running', in P. Norton (ed.), *Parliaments and Governments in Western Europe* (London and Portland, OR: Frank Cass, 1998).
3. Shephard, 'The European Parliament'.
4. *General Report on the Activities of the European Union* (Brussels: EC Commission, 1996, p.422).
5. *EuroMP: Weekly Newsletter*, 9 June 1997 and 7 July 1997.
6. For a detailed listing see Shephard, 'The European Parliament'.
7. Committee on Petitions, *Report on the Rights of Disabled People*, 21 Nov. 1996, Text A4-0391/96, pp.9–17.
8. Committee of Inquiry into the Community Transit System, Hearing XIV, 18 Nov. 1996: Part II. Evidence given by the tobacco industry.
9. R. Corbett, F. Jacobs and M. Shackleton, *The European Parliament* (London: Cartermill, 1995), p.275.
10. J. Tomlinson MEP, *Sports Intergroup – Background*, 13 Feb. 1996.
11. Conference outline, *Conference of the European Parliament and Local Authorities of the European Union*, Brussels, 1–3 Oct. 1996.
12. *General Report on the Activities of the European Union* (EC Commission: Brussels, 1996, p.421).
13. B. Hagard, *Sports Intergroup – European Parliament Report for DGX*, 13 Feb. 1996.
14. *European Parliament: The Week*, 22 Oct. 1997 and 18 Nov. 1997.
15. S.S. Andersen and K.A. Eliassen, 'European Community Lobbying', *European Journal of Political Research*, Vol.20 (1991), p.175.
16. *EP News*, 15–19 Jan. 1996, p.2.
17. Several of these findings were first reported in, M. Shephard, 'The European Parliament: Laying the Foundations for Awareness and Support', *Parliamentary Affairs*, Vol.50 (1997), pp.438–52.
18. *EuroMP: Weekly Newsletter*, 7 April 1997.
19. Corbett, Jacobs and Shackleton, *The European Parliament*, p.281.
20. See for example, J. Greenwood, 'EU Decision-Making and Channels of Influence', in J. Greenwood, *Representing Interests in the European Union* (New York: St. Martin's Press, 1997), p.27.
21. K. Butler, 'MEPs Ban Gifts in Bid for High Ground', *The Independent*, 18 July 1996, p.12.
22. See Greenwood, 'The Regulation of Interest Representation', in Greenwood, *Representing Interests in the European Union*. pp.83–4.
23. See E. de Bony, 'Lobbying the EU: the Search for Ground Rules', *European Trends. The Economist Intelligence Unit*. London, No.3 (1994), pp.73–9.
24. See J. Greenwood, 'The Regulation of Interest Representation', pp.85–6.
25. Greenwood, 'The Regulation of Interest Representation', p.87.
26. Yves Galland was the initial appointment as rapporteur, but had to relinquish his position when he was appointed to a government position in France.
27. European Parliament Committee on the Rules of Procedure, the Verification of Credentials and Immunities, *Report on Lobbying in the European Parliament*, 27 Sept. 1995, DOC_EN\RR\282\282679, p.9.
28. *Report on Lobbying in the European Parliament*.
29. *Report on Lobbying in the European Parliament*.
30. *Report on Lobbying in the European Parliament*, p.4.
31. *Report on Lobbying in the European Parliament*, p.7.
32. European Parliament Committee on the Rules of Procedure, the Verification of

Credentials and Immunities, *Report on the Amendment of Annex I of the Rules of Procedure Concerning Transparency and Members' Financial Interests*, 27 Sept. 1995, DOC_EN\RR\282\282681, p.8.
33. On-Line News Briefs from the Green Group in the European Parliament. Highlights of the 15 to 19 January 1996 Plenary Session in Strasbourg, *Lobbying*.
34. G. Ford, 'Travelling with Phantoms', *The House Magazine*, 29 Jan. 1996, p.14; and *The European Parliament: The Week*, 15–19 Jan. 1996, p.24.
35. *EP News*, 15–19 Jan. 1996. p.2.
36. *EP News*, 15–19 Jan. 1996, p.3.
37. *EP News*, 15–19 Jan. 1996, p.2.
38. *European Parliament: Rules of Procedure*, Annex 1, 19 Feb. 1997.
39. European Parliament Committee on the Rules of Procedure, the Verification of Credentials and Immunities, *Report on the Code of Conduct Governing Lobbyists*, 21 March 1997, Text A4-0107/97, pp.4–7.
40. *Verbatim Report of Proceedings (Provisional Edition)*, 12/05/97, May part session 1997, Amendment to Rules (code of conduct for lobbyists), 1-045.
41. J. Greenwood, 'The Regulation of Interest Representation', p.98.

CHAPTER 9

Conclusion: Conflicting Pressures

PHILIP NORTON

The relationship between parliaments and pressure groups is as complex as it is under-explored. What emerges from the preceding chapters is a web of relationships that has been little studied, especially in a comparative context. The chapters provide a fascinating insight into the links between parliament and organised interests in each country as well as providing the basis for generalising about the relationship between parliaments and interest groups. The generalisations necessarily must be tentative, given that the country coverage is selective rather than exhaustive, but they help further our understanding of parliaments and provide the impetus for further research.

TARGETS AND CHANNELS

In terms of our two basic hypotheses, the material provided in the country-specific chapters provides support for both, though with qualifications. Our first hypothesis, that parliaments have been forced largely to operate at the deliberative stage of the policy cycle, has been supported by a preceding study and by this one.[1] As parliaments respond to what governments bring forward, the focus of group attention is government, not parliament. The exceptions to this are those legislatures that are not confined to the deliberative stage of the policy cycle and exercise some independent capacity to generate and substitute policy of their own: in other words, policy-making legislatures or those which come close to occupying that category. The most obvious example in a global context is the United States.[2] In the context of our study, the exception is Italy (Chapter 4). Other legislatures may exercise some influence over policy, but it is exercised primarily in response to what the executive brings forward.

The second hypothesis flows in part from the second. Given that parliaments are not policy-making bodies, we would not expect them to be primary targets of pressure group activity in the political system. Given that they can exert some influence at the deliberative stage, we would expect them to be targets to a limited degree. However, as parliaments are authoritative bodies that meet in plenary session, and usually enjoy a proximity to government-denied groups, we would expect them to be utilised more regularly by pressure groups as channels rather than targets. This again is largely supported by the evidence in this volume, though with qualifications. The Italian Parliament is a target and a channel. Other parliaments are principally channels. Organised interests recognise the value of lobbying parliaments in order to get their case on the public record and as a means of reaching government as well as the public. As we have seen, parliaments frequently make use of committees to consider and report on proposals for changes in public policy. Groups send in evidence to these committees and may be invited to appear before them. Committee hearings are variously utilised by groups to get their voices heard in the UK Parliament (Chapter 2), the German Bundestag (Chapter 3) and the European Parliament (Chapter 8). Furthermore, in all three parliaments there has been a growth in this activity. Groups recognise the value of putting their views on the public record. The incentive to exploit this opportunity is greatest for outsider groups, as is apparent in the case of Germany, though insider groups are also likely to exploit the opportunity, especially where they have no formalised or direct links with parliamentary parties or members of the legislature.

The experience of Germany also leads us to draw an important distinction in terms of the relationship between parliaments and pressure groups. Though the use of parliament as a channel by interest groups is a common feature of legislatures, the extent to which groups need to exploit it as such differs. It differs according to whether the relationship between groups and other actors in the political system is direct and

CONCLUSION

formalised or indirect and not highly formalised. Parliaments may be located on a spectrum, at one end with a political system where groups and actors have a highly formalised relationship and at the other where there is no such relationship, groups standing at some distance from both the government and the parliament. Of the countries covered in this volume, Germany, Belgium and the Netherlands come closest to being at the former end of the spectrum. The United Kingdom is closest to the other end of the spectrum. It does not fall, though, at the very end. There are links between organised interests and some members of parliament, and some formal links between groups and parties (as with the trades unions and the Labour Party), but government and parliament are generally regarded as being largely autonomous of interest groups. The other countries, such as Italy and Ireland, as well as the European Parliament, fall somewhere along the spectrum, perhaps closer to the mid-point.

In countries such as Belgium, where there are fairly structured links between groups and political actors, groups do not have such a great incentive as in other countries to utilise parliament as a channel to government, because they already have a direct channel of their own. Though parliament in each case is still used as a channel, insider groups are under less pressure to use it as such than those outsider groups that do not have formal links with parliamentary parties or individual members. In countries where there are no such strong, formalised links, there is a greater incentive for groups of all types to utilise parliaments as channels.

This finding leads to another – one that is largely intuitive. Where a parliament exercises some independent capacity to affect outcomes, we would expect it to be a target of pressure group lobbying. Where pressure groups enjoy no strong formalised links with government or political parties, we would expect the parliament to be lobbied by groups keen to exploit it as a channel for reaching political actors. What emerges from the contributions to this volume is that those parliaments which fall into these categories have also experienced problems in the relationship between pressure groups and members of parliament, and demands for the greater regulation of that relationship. In Italy, where parliament is a target of pressure group activity, the demands have formed but part of a response to a wider systemic problem. Elsewhere, in Ireland and the United Kingdom, as well as the European Parliament, the demands for regulation have been in response to the perceived exploitation by parliamentarians of the opportunity to enrich themselves in return for pursuing the cause of particular groups. There has been no comparable pressure, and no obvious public concern, in the case of those parliaments at the other end of the spectrum.

One other generalisation can also be drawn from the contributions to this volume, and that is that the relationship between groups and parliaments is dynamic. In some cases, parliaments have grown in significance, either as targets or channels, whereas in some countries they have declined in significance. In the case of the European Parliament, the Parliament has become more attractive to groups as it has become a more central player in the European law-making process. As we have seen (Chapter 8), it is also likely to become more attractive as more treaty provisions are brought within the co-operation or co-decision procedure. In the Netherlands and Germany, parliament has if anything declined in significance as groups have lost their hold over parliamentary parties or members of parliament. In Germany, the rise of the career politician has had a very different effect to that which it has had in Britain: it has served to displace interest group representatives as members of the Bundestag. The parliament thus loses some of its appeal to groups, especially insider groups, who come to rely even more on their links with government. In the Netherlands, the move towards a more pluralist society, emphasising the primacy of politics, has served to create a similar effect, representatives of interest groups being pushed out of parliament. The emphasis is far more on parties, and parties, according to Rinus Van Schendelen (Chapter 6), are declining in importance, leaving groups to focus on the executive.

CONSEQUENCES

We hypothesised that the relationship between groups and parliaments would have positive as well as negative consequences. We surmised that there would be positive consequences for groups (in terms of achieving action on their

CONCLUSION

behalf), for parliamentarians (obtaining information), and for the political system (bolstering support). The evidence from the preceding chapters tends to support these hypotheses.

Interest groups benefit from their contacts with parliaments in that on occasion they can influence a change in decision by parliamentarians and, more regularly and pervasively, through members of parliament they can make their views known to ministers and officials and to the mass media and public. Parliaments may not often exercise a significant decision-making capacity but they can offer a useful platform. This is apparent from the contributions to this volume. Groups in many countries use the opportunities to publicise their case through parliament. They may use parliament to publicise an issue already on the political agenda or they may even succeed in getting parliamentarians to engage in some element of agenda setting. Vincent Della Sala (Chapter 4) has recorded the example of several groups succeeding in finally getting a debate in the Italian Chamber of Deputies in 1995 on family policy, despite an unwillingness on the part of the parties to raise it. Groups ask members of parliament to raise issues through making speeches, introducing private members' bills (where provision for introducing such bills exists, as in Italy and Britain), and asking questions. In both Italy and Britain, oral questions are useful as a means of attracting publicity. Groups also send written material to committees and may attend hearings of the committees. Indeed, as we have noted already, there is a growing use of committees by groups. This activity suggests that groups perceive some benefit for themselves. Though, as we shall see, there may be costs in terms of resources (staff time, hiring lobbyists), the benefits in terms of making one's voice heard through a formal authoritative forum – the nation's elected assembly – outweighs the costs.

Parliamentarians also benefit from the input provided by interest groups. Groups constitute an important source of information. Parliaments have limited resources. For information and guidance, they are heavily dependent on government and, as far as most members are concerned, on political parties. Information provided by interest groups can be valuable to members, especially opposition members. Whereas government has the support of a bureaucracy, opposition parties have no such support, or at least nothing on a comparable scale. In the German Bundestag, one-quarter of the members of a committee can require a public hearing. This provides the opportunity for the major opposition party to force hearings and, as Thomas Saalfeld notes (Chapter 3), public hearings are most frequently initiated by the opposition parties. Members may not only utilise information sent to them by groups, they may actively solicit it. Mention was made in Chapter 2 of a study of the passage through the British House of Commons of the Financial Services Bill. Members of the standing committee dealing with the bill not only were sent masses of unsolicited material, but a number organised meetings with interested groups.[3]

The third hypothesis also finds some support in our findings. Where groups enjoy access to parliament, and are able to utilise that access for the purposes of influencing parliamentary deliberations and making their voice heard, we would expect them to be more supportive of the political system than if such access was denied them. It is clear from the studies in this volume that groups make substantial use of access to parliaments. Those groups that do not make much use of it include, in the German case, insider groups, who enjoy close relationships to government departments and, given that relationship, are hardly likely to be critics of the political system. For outsider groups, those not having regular access to government, parliament offers a means – albeit imperfect and sometimes unresponsive – of getting one's views on the formal political record. In Germany, for example, environmental groups have been able to get their views on the record, through parliamentary hearings, as a consequence of the Green Party's presence since 1983 in the Bundestag. As long as parliaments appear relevant to groups as targets or channels there appears relatively little use of extra-parliamentary means to agitate and get their views heard; but where parliaments do not seem greatly relevant groups sometimes deploy extra-parliamentary means to make their voices heard. The use made of parliaments by pressure groups thus appears to contribute to political stability.

However, some of these positive effects are qualified by the negative consequences we hypothesised would result from the contact pressure groups have with parliaments. The evidence of this volume tends to support, directly or by inference, the hypotheses we advanced: namely, that lobbying is likely to be an ineffective means of influencing outcomes, that information flowing to parliamentarians may be skewed or tainted, that increasing lobbying may result in an overload of work for parliamentarians, and that close links between groups and parliamentarians may serve to undermine popular support for the political system.

The evidence to support the first hypothesis is limited and can only be inferred from the country studies and from evidence of other works. It applies primarily in the case of parliament as a target rather than parliament as a channel. In those cases where pressure groups target parliaments, they do so in order to influence outcomes. What is apparent from the country studies is the extent to which party still holds sway in parliaments, providing voting cues and in most cases determining the outcomes. Where groups enjoy the status of insider groups, they are not likely to need to target parliament. Outsider groups may employ their resources to target parliament but by virtue of being outsiders are not likely to overturn decisions already made by government. This applies principally in the case of reactive, or policy-influencing, legislatures. As we have seen, lobbying is more likely to be effective where parliaments do have some independent capacity to affect outcomes, notably in the case of Italy and, to a lesser extent, in the case of the European Parliament which, in terms of categorising legislatures, is *sui generis*.

The evidence to support the second hypothesis is more substantial. Information supplied to parliaments by groups will almost always be self-serving. It may also be skewed or tainted. That is, it may be one-sided, a particular group or interest dominating the input, or it may be presented in a misleading way. We have seen evidence of particular groups dominating in those parliaments where there is a direct and close link between groups and parties or individual members. We also have some evidence of groups dominating the input on some occasions in other parliament. Eunan O'Halpin (Chapter 7) records the case in Ireland of the Joint Committee on Small Businesses (1983–87) which allowed itself 'to become largely dependent for research support and topics of inquiry on a unit of the (then) Confederation of Irish Industry, and produced a long succession of reports which were little more than partisan small business wish lists'. Tainted information may also flow from parliamentarians who enjoy close links, sometimes remunerated links, with outside groups. As we have seen, there have been demands, variously acted upon, for members of some parliaments to be subject to rules requiring disclosure, or a limitation, of such links.

The evidence of the country chapters also provides some support, though largely by inference, for the third hypothesis, that increased lobbying may result in parliamentarians being overloaded with work. Lobbying of parliamentarians has increased in recent years, notably so in the case of Britain, Ireland and the European Parliament. Lobbying requires a response by parliamentarians. That response may have political costs. It also has a cost in terms of time and resources. We have seen in the case of Britain that meetings with representatives of interest groups is a time-consuming activity, as is the task of simply opening mail sent by groups. The demands made of members is also clear from the evidence presented by Eunan O'Halpin in the case of Ireland, where pressure group lobbying has increased especially at the local level. Of questions asked in the Dail in May 1997, about half of those dealing with constituency issues reflected the concerns of local pressure groups rather than individual constituents. As O'Halpin records, 'it seems reasonable to predict that, as pressure group politics mushroom, so TDs will have to spend even more of their time in propiating these powerful if sometimes transient local forces'. In parliaments where members are already busy, spending more time responding to lobbying by pressure groups has an opportunity cost: it may be at the expense of responding to the grievances of individual citizens or engaging in scrutiny of government on behalf of the electorate.

The fourth hypothesis, as we have already seen, has to be qualified. There is evidence to suggest that popular support for the political system is threatened as a consequence of perceived overly close links between individual parliamentarians and particular groups. However, this does not apply in the case of all parliaments. Those parliaments which can be located more towards what may be termed the pluralist end of the spectrum have experienced this problem. Those which fall more towards the corporatist end, notably Germany, have not. The explanation

CONCLUSION

for this difference can be located in the political culture of the nation and the structures and relationships that flow from that culture. A liberal, or highly pluralistic, culture emphasises the individual and the role of government as arbiter, whereas a more corporatist culture emphasises social organisations and views government as but one actor in the process of determining public policy. An intimate and formalised relationship between government and interest groups is viewed as largely illegitimate in the former and as proper in the latter. By extension, close links between members of parliament and outside groups are viewed as suspect in the former but as natural in the latter.

CONCLUSIONS

Parliamentary activity cannot be understood without some reference to interest groups, yet it is remarkable how little attention the relationship between parliaments and interest groups has received. Scholars concerned with policy analysis have tended to focus, quite legitimately, on the relationship of governments and groups, since it is governments, alone or in consultation or formal collaboration with organised interests, that usually 'make' public policy. However, parliaments in western Europe have some contact with interest groups. It is a two-way relationship. Parliaments have something to offer groups (a capacity, albeit usually rarely exercised, to decide outcomes, a valuable platform, and in some cases legitimacy) and groups have something to offer parliaments (advice, information and, in some cases, legitimacy). Parliaments are targets and, more frequently, channels for pressure groups intent on achieving a change in public policy. As targets, they are mostly, though not wholly, secondary to government. Their primary and pervasive attraction to groups is as a means of reaching government and getting their views on the public record.

The relationship between parliament and interest groups varies from parliament to parliament and over time. There are, as we have seen, negative as well as positive consequences to the lobbying of parliaments by pressure groups; in some cases, there have been scandals over the links between individual parliamentarians and particular pressure groups. However, what is clear from this study is that contact between interest groups and parliaments takes place usually (though not in all cases) on a fairly substantial scale, occupying a significant amount of time of parliamentarians and parliamentary committees, and that such contact is hardly likely to disappear. Indeed, it would not be in the interests of either side for it to disappear. In some polities that exhibit liberal cultures there is some pressure for greater regulation of the contact that takes place between members of parliament and organised interests, but that pressure is to ensure transparency and greater equity in access to members; it is not designed to close off access to the elected assembly.

What we have identified is a symbiotic and significant relationship, one variously overlooked by those focusing on executive–legislative relations and on policy making. Parliaments in western Europe cannot be understood without reference to their relationship to organised interests. The significance of that relationship is demonstrated by the intent of the new democracies of central and eastern Europe to develop civil society, with myriad non-governmental organisations and with those organisations having the capacity to develop links with and to lobby government and parliament.[4] Interest groups are a feature of a free society and part of that freedom entails the opportunity to make representations to members of the national parliament. That freedom is employed widely, and in some cases extensively, in the countries of western Europe, usually to the benefit of parliaments as well as the groups. Too much should not be made of the relationship in terms of direct policy making, but the significance of it in terms of influencing policy deliberations, generating public debate and informing parliament deserves acknowledgement.

NOTES

1. P. Norton (ed.), *Parliaments and Governments in Western Europe* (London and Portland, OR: Frank Cass, 1998).
2. See M. Mezey, *Comparative Legislatures* (Durham, NC: Duke University Press, 1979).
3. P. Norton, 'Public Legislation', in M. Rush (ed.), *Parliament and Pressure Politics* (Oxford: Clarendon Press, 1990), p.197.
4. See D.M. Olson and P. Norton (eds.), *The New Parliaments of Central and Eastern Europe* (London and Portland, OR: Frank Cass, 1996).

Index

abortion, 9, 125
advocacy, 15, 34, 36
Agricultural Policy, Federal Committee for, 45
Agnelli, Gianni, 70
agricultural groups, 20, 50, 53, 63, 70, 81, 89, 101, 112, 114, 115, 126
Ahern, Bertie, 124
Aitken, Jonathan, 35
amendments, 9, 21, 25, 26, 32, 58, 84, 96, 98, 111, 114, 154
Amsterdam Treaty, 146, 147
Andersen, S.S., 152
Anonymous Empire, 22
Appropriations Committee, 57, 58
Association of Christian-Democratic Students, 45
Association of Christian Democrats in Local Government, 45
Association of Employees' Affairs, 46
Association of Expellees and Refugees, 45
Association of Persecuted Social Democrats, 46
Association of Professional Political Consultants (APPC), 38
Association of Social Democratic Lawyers, 46
Association of Social Democratic Women, 46
Association of Social Democrats in the Health Sector, 46
Automobile Association ('AA'), 14

baby seal, product ban, 148
Bank of Ireland, 132
Banotti, Mary, 149
'bargained pluralism', 71
Belgium, 88–109, 169
benefits, 11–13
Berlusconi, Silvio, 70

Bishop of Galway, 125
Bjerregard, Ritt, 161
Breathnach, Niamh, 136
Britain – see United Kingdom
Bruton, John, 139
budget committee, 15, 86, 149
budgetary process, 82–5, 102
Bundesrat, 58
Bundestag, 43–66, 168, 170, 172
Burke, Ray, 127, 141–2
business and commerce, 19, 20, 22, 25, 45, 46, 50, 52, 53, 55, 58, 59, 63, 81, 91, 101, 112, 115–16, 120, 126
Business and Employers Confederation, Ireland, 132

Cabinet Office, the, 38
career politicians, 30, 31, 47–8
'cash for questions' scandal, 35, 36
caucus, 58
cause groups, 3, 4, 19, 50, 52, 59
Christian Democratic Employees, 45
Christian Democratic Party (Belgium, French-Speaking), 93
Christian Democratic Union (CDU), 45, 46, 47, 53–7, 58, 61
Christian Democrats, 69
Christian-Democratic Students, Association of, 45
Christian Democrats in Local Government, Association of, 45
Christian Social Union (CSU), 45, 46, 47, 53–7, 58, 61
churches, 27, 53
civil rights, 20, 46, 78
civil service, 63, 116–20
closure motions, 75
coalition, 124
COBAS, 70
code of conduct, 36, 38, 159
co-decision procedure, 146–7

177

Coldiretti, 70
College of Quaestors, 159
Committee of Petitions, 149
Committee on Foreign Affairs, 133
Committee on Rules of Procedure, 156
Committee on Standards in Public Life, 36, 37–8, 159
Committee on Women's Rights, Joint Oireachatas, 133
committee stage, 21, 26, 57–8
committees, 10, 13, 15, 25, 26, 29–30, 32, 33, 39, 49, 57–61, 75, 81, 85, 95–6, 98, 103, 114, 133, 149–50
Communist Party, 69, 71, 78
Communist Refoundation, 69
'concertation', 69
Confederation of Irish Industry, 133, 173
Congress, US, xii, 12, 21
Connolly, Eileen, 124–44
Conservative Party, the, 21, 23, 27, 28, 36
Conservatives (Netherlands), 110, 118
constitution, 67, 72, 73, 78, 82
consultancies, 23, 27, 29, 30–31, 38
consultation procedure, 146–7
consumer groups, 115
Convention of Royal Burghs, the, 19
cooperation procedure, 146–7
corporatism, 67, 69
Corruption and Misconduct in Contemporary British Politics, 34
Council for the Status of Women, 134

Dail (Ireland), 124, 128, 133, 174
de Tocqueville, Alexis, 1
de Winter, Lieven, 88–109
Debuyst, F., 91
decisional functions, 8
'deferred bribes', 16
Della Sala, Vincent, 67–87, 171
Democratic Left party, 142
Desert Act, 120
Di Palma, Giuseppe, 73
Disability Forum, European, 149
disarmament groups, 115
divorce, 130
Dod's Parliamentary Companion, 23
Donnelly, Brendan, 163
drugs, 78
Dunnes Stores, 140

early day motions, 33, 39
Economic Affairs Committee, 58
Economic and Monetary Union, 86, 119

Economic Council, 45
education sector, 89, 101
Electoral Act, 142
Eliassen, K.A., 152
Employees' Affairs, Association of, 46
Employees' Group, 55, 57
employer groups, *see* business
enquiry commissions, 60
environmental groups, 46, 54, 71, 92, 115, 120, 129
Environment, Public Health and Consumer Protection Committee, 149
Ethics in Public Office Act, 139, 142
Euro MP, 154
European Affairs Committee, 57
European Confederation of Tobacco Retailers, 150
European Disability Forum, 149
European Parliament, 11, 145–66, 168, 170, 173, 174
European People's Party (EPP), 160
Expellees and Refugees, Association of, 45

Family Committee, 58
famine, 78
Farmers Association, 58
farming, *see* agricultural groups
Federal Committee for Agricultural Policy, 45
Federal Employment Office, 43
Fianna Fail, 132, 139
Fiat strike, 70
Finance Bill, 27, 83
Finance Committee, 58
financial links, 22, 34, 37, 38, 100, 115, 126–7, 139
Financial Services Bill, 26, 172
Fine Gael, 139
Finer, S.E., 21, 22, 27
Fitzgerald, G., 129
Flemish Christian Democratic Party, 89, 92
Flemish Nationalist Party, 94
Ford, Glyn, 158–62
Foreign Affairs, Committee on, 133
Forza Italia, 70, 81
Free Democratic Party (FDP), 46, 54, 55, 62

Gallagher, Michael, 135
Galle, Marc, 156
Galway, Bishop of, 125

INDEX

Garda Representative Association, 132
Germany, 43–66, 168, 169, 170, 172
GJW (political consultancy), 23
Grant, Wyn, 3, 4, 19, 68, 90
Green Group (EP), 160
Green Party (Belgium), 94
Green Party (Germany), 46, 47, 62, 172
Green, Pauline, 160
Greer, Ian, 23, 36
Group of Deputies Representing Expellees and Refugees, 56

Hamilton, Neil, 36
Haughey, Charles, 127, 140–42
Healey, Denis, 20
Health Affairs Committee, 58
health sector, 89, 101
Herzog, Dietrich, 49, 62
Hine, David, 71, 83
Hirner, Manfred, 53
homosexuality, 9, 27
House of Commons (UK), 10, 19–42, 62, 79, 133, 159, 172
House of Lords (UK), 26, 30
House of Representatives (Belgium), 91
human rights, 148

immigration, 9
industrialisation, 5, 7, 19
information provision, 5, 12, 32, 39, 58, 60, 79, 96, 130–31, 154, 171, 173
insider groups, 3–5, 6, 9–10, 19–20, 60, 62, 67, 68, 90–91
'interest-group islands', 58
Intergovernmental Conference (IGC) Ireland, 124–44
'internal lobby', 45, 61
Ireland, 124–44, 170, 173, 174
Irish Business and Employers Confederation, 132
Irish Congress of Trade Unions, 132
Irish Tobacco Manufacturers' Advisory Committee, 132
Ismayr, Wolfgang, 47–8
Italian Women's Union (UDI), 71
Italy, 67–87, 168, 171, 173

Jenkins, Roy, 133
Joint Committee on Small Businesses, 133, 173
Joint Oireachatas Committee on Women's Rights, 133
Justice Committee, 57

Katzenstein, Peter J., 43
Klein, Rudolf, 5

Labour and Social Affairs Committee, 58
Labour Party, the, 20, 34, 36, 38, 169
land mines, 148
Landtag, 49
legislation; deliberation, 8, 59, 125, 145, 172; drafting, 9, 57, 77, 98; formulation, 8, 145; initiation, 6, 8, 9, 49, 96, 111, 145
Lehne, Klaus-Heiner, 163
Liberals, 89, 94
lobbying, 2, 5, 8, 9–10, 14, 23, 24, 26–7, 29, 31–8, 68, 117, 130–32
'lobby list', 49
Local Government Affairs, Social Democratic Association for, 46
Lower House (Netherlands), 110
Lowry, Michael, 127, 139–41

Maastricht Treaty, 69, 82, 146
mail, 10, 24, 25, 27, 132, 152
Major, John, 35
Mandela, Nelson, 148
manufacturing, 5
maternity benefits, 73
McAleese, Mary, 126
media, 9, 31, 49, 81, 90
Members' Interests, Select Committee on, 24, 34, 35
Mezey, Michael, 7
Middle Class Association, 45
Middle Class Discussion Circle, 56, 57
mobilisation, 9, 99
Modernisation of the House of Commons, Select Committee on, 39
monetary policy, 81
monopoly, 5
motions, 25, 39, 114
motivation (of MPs), 22, 64
MPs for Hire, 34

National Army Spouse's Association, 137
National Farmers' Union, 20
National Health Insurance Act, 19
'neo-corporatism', 43–4, 52–3, 88, 104, 128
Netherlands, 110–23, 169, 170
Nolan, Lord, 35, 159
Nordmann, Jean-Thomas, 158–61
Norton, Philip, 1–18, 19–42, 44, 72, 167–76

179

Nutrition, Agriculture and Forestry Standing Committee, 58

O'Halpin, Eunan, 124–44, 173
Open Market 1992 programme, 118
'organised pluralism', 62
'outliers', 96
outsider groups, 3–5, 13, 14, 60, 68, 71, 173
overload (of material), 15

Packenham, Robert, 8
Palace of Westminster, 24
Pannella, Marco, 78
'parapublic institutions', 43
Parliamentary Commissioner for Administration, 36, 38
parliaments, as 'targets' or 'channels', 8, 22, 29, 39, 44, 61, 67, 68, 72, 77, 168, 173, 175
parties, 7, 9, 13, 31, 44, 45–9, 53–7, 58, 88, 103–4, 134–5
partitocracy, 88
Party of Democratic Socialism, 55
Party of European Socialists, *see* Socialist Group
pension reform, 69
Petitions, Committee of, 149
pluralism/pluralist theory, 1, 14, 52, 59, 67, 71, 89, 174
policy communities, 6, 31, 60, 116–17, 118, 121
political consultants, *see* consultants, also lobbying
popular support, 15, 173
Poulson, John, 34
pressure group, definition, 2, 110
'primacy of politics', 119–21
private legislation, 20
private members' legislation, 9, 21, 39, 72–3, 75, 77–8, 96, 98, 171
professional groups, 19, 20
Professional Political Consultants, Association of (APPC), 38
Pro-Life Amendment Committee, 129
'Pro-Life Campaign', 129
promotional groups, *see* cause groups
public policy, 1–2, 3, 5, 20
publicity, 9, 31, 49, 81, 90
Pupils' Union, 45

Quaestors, College of, 159
questions (in parliament), 10, 14, 22, 25, 26, 30, 33, 35, 37, 39, 68, 81, 96–7, 102, 114, 131, 136, 151
quorum, 75

Radical Party, 78
Radio and Television Broadcasting Committee, 81
Rape Crisis Centres, 133
rapporteurs, 57, 158
reactive legislatures, 7, 8
recruitment, 91–5
referendums, 78–9, 126, 130
Register of MPs' Interests, 31, 34, 97, 139
regulation, 28, 154, 156–7
religious groups, 20, 50, 78, 89, 92, 110, 115
Report on Parliamentary Assistants, 163
report stage, 26
Research and Technology Committee, 58
research staff, 12, 33, 35, 56, 97–9, 104, 114, 163, 173
resources, 14, 32, 56, 97–9, 121, 155–6, 171
Reynolds, Albert, 127
Richards, Peter G., 22
Roman Catholic Church, 125
Rothmans, 150
Rules of Procedure, Committee on, 156
Russell Greer, 23

Saalfeld, Thomas, 43–66, 172
'safety valve', 13
Sakharov prize, 148
salaries, 30, 114
Schmid, Josef, 45
Seanad (Ireland), 124, 137
Sebaldt, Martin, 62
secrecy, 22, 95, 113
secret ballot, 73
sectional groups, 3, 4, 19, 21, 50, 52, 75, 83
Select Committee on Members' Interests, 24, 34, 35
Select Committee on Modernisation of the House of Commons, 39
Select Committee on Standards and Privileges, 36
Senior Citizens' Union, 45
Shephard, Mark P., 145–66
Shops Bill, 27, 29
Single European Act 1987, 118, 145
Small Businesses, Joint Committee on, 133, 173

INDEX

Social Democratic Association for Local Government Affairs, 46
Social Democratic Lawyers, Association of, 46
Social Democratic Women, Association of, 46
Social Democrats (SPD), 45, 46, 47, 53–7, 61
Social Democrats, Association of Persecuted, 46
Social Democrats in the Health Sector, Association of, 46
Socialist Group (EP), 154–5, 160
Socialist Party (Netherlands), 110, 115
Socialists (Belgium), 89, 93
Socialists (Italy), 69
Society for the Protection of the Unborn Child, 129
special standing committees, 39
Spiers, Shaun, 163
Stock Exchange, 39
strikes and protests, 69, 84
Standards and Privileges, Select Committee on, 36
Standards in Public Life, Committee on, 36, 37–8, 159
students' groups, 71
Sunday Times, 35
Sunday trading, 27
Suu Kyi, Aung San, 148

taxation, 9, 20, 128
televised proceedings, 30, 131
'Ten Commandments', 157
Thatcher, Margaret, 29, 128
Tobacco Manufacturers' Advisory Committee, Irish, 132
Trade Board Acts, 19
trade unions, 5, 19, 20, 27, 28, 45, 50–55, 58, 61, 63, 67–9, 71, 81, 89, 91, 93–4, 114–15, 117, 120, 126, 132, 169
Trades Union Congress (TUC); UK, 30; Ireland, 132
trading, Sunday, 27
traffic regulation, 136
Transport Committee, 58, 149
turnout, 125

United Kingdom, 14, 19–42, 168, 169, 171, 174
United States, 1, 16, 167
Upper House (Netherlands), 111

Van Schendelen, M.P.C.M., 110–23, 170
vigils, 27
Vlaams Blok (extreme right) Party, 94

wage indexation, 70
Walkland, Stuart, 21
welfare state, 77
Westminster Babylon, 34
Westminster, Palace of, 24
Westminster Strategy (political consultancy), 23
Women Committee, 58
Women's Association, 45
Women's Group, 56, 57
women's groups, 71, 78, 92, 129
Women's Political Association, 134
women's rights, 133
Women's Union (UDI), Italy, 71
Working Group for Local Government Affairs, 56
Working Group of Protestant Christian Democrats, 45

Young Socialists, 46
Young Union, 45
Youth Committee, 58

Library of Legislative Studies
Series Editor: Philip Norton, *University of Hull*

The New Roles of Parliamentary Committees

Lawrence D Longley, *Lawrence University, USA* and **Roger H Davidson**, *University of Maryland* (Eds)

Parliaments had widely been expected to decline in significance in the later part of the twentieth century, but instead they have developed new and vital political roles and have innovated in their institutional structure – most recurrently in newly organised or invigorated parliamentary committees, not only in a few parliaments but as a global phenomenon.

This publication is devoted to the study and evaluation of these important and still emergent parliamentary developments – to an understanding of the new roles of parliamentary committees in the quest for effective parliamentary influence in and contribution to democratic government.

Contents: Parliamentary Committees: Changing Perspectives on Changing Institutions *Lawrence D. Longley and Roger H. Davidson*. Parliamentary Committees in European Democracies *Kaare Strøm*. Norwegian Parliamentary Committees: Performance, Structural Change and External Relations *Hilmar Rommetvedt*. Changing Parliamentary Committees in Changing East-Central Europe: Parliamentary Committees as Central Sites of Policy Making *Attila Ágh*. Committees in the Post-Communist Polish Sejm: Structure, Activity and Members *David M. Olson, Ania van der Meer-Krok-Paszkowska, Maurice D. Simon and Irena Jackiewicz*. US Congressional Committees: Changing Legislative Workshops *Colton C. Campbell and Roger H. Davidson*. Nascent Institutionalisation: Committees in the British Parliament *Philip Norton*. Political Reform and the Committee System in Israel: Structural and Functional Adaptation *Reuven Y. Hazan*. Committees in the Russian State Duma: Continuity and Change in Comparative Perspective *Moshe Haspel*. The Organisation and Workings of Committees in the Korean National Assembly *Chan Wook Park*. Parliamentary Committees: A Global Perspective *Malcolm Shaw*.

264 pages   1998
0 7146 4891 4 cloth   0 7146 4442 0   paper
A special issue of The Journal of Legislative Studies

Parliaments in *Contemporary Western Europe*

General Editor: Philip Norton, *University of Hull*

The attention given to new parliaments has not been matched by a study of established parliaments. This series fills that gap. It draws together studies of a number of West European parliaments and it provides an accessible study of relationships not previously studied in depth.

Parliaments and Governments in Western Europe

Philip Norton (Ed)

The relationship between parliament and government is fundamental to a political system. In this volume, a distinguished team of specialists explores that relationship and considers to what extent parliaments have the capacity to constrain governments. Are there particular institutional features, such as specialisation through committees, that enhance their capacity to influence public policy?
Volume 1   232 pages   1998
0 7146 4833 7 cloth   0 7146 4385 8 paper

Parliaments and Citizens in Western Europe

Philip Norton (Ed)

Citizens elect the parliament, but what contact takes place between citizen and parliament in between elections? The authors assess the extent and nature of that contact.
Volume 3   172 pages   1999
0 7146 4835 3 cloth   0 7146 4387 4 paper

FRANK CASS PUBLISHERS
Newbury House, 900 Eastern Avenue, Newbury Park, Ilford, Essex IG2 7HH
Tel: +44 (0)181 599 8866 Fax: +44 (0)181 599 0984 E-mail: info@frankcass.com
NORTH AMERICA
c/o ISBS, 5804 NE Hassalo Street, Portland, OR 97213 3644, USA
Tel: 1 800 944 6190 Fax: 503 280 8732 E-mail: cass@isbs.com
Website: http://www.frankcass.com

National Parliaments and the European Union

Philip Norton, *University of Hull* (Ed)

This is a solid comparative collection, providing up-to-date and in-depth illustration of the potential, and problems, involved in thinking about parliamentary democracy in established EU member countries.'
International Affairs

This volume is the first to study in depth how national parliaments have adapted to the effects of the Single European Act and the Maastricht Treaty. Detailed studies of ten parliaments allow generalisations to be drawn about national parliaments – how they have adapted, or not adapted, to European integration.

198 pages 1996
0 7146 4691 1 cloth 0 7146 4330 0 paper
A special issue of The Journal of Legislative Studies

The New Parliaments of Central and Eastern Europe

David M. Olson, *University of North Carolina* and
Philip Norton, *University of Hull* (Eds)

What role have parliaments played in the dramatic changes occurring in eastern and central Europe? Adopting a common research framework, the contributors analyse in detail the role and operations of parliaments in ten of the new democracies. They focus on what determines their capacity to have some impact on public policy.

254 pages 1996 0 7146 4715 2 cloth 0 7146 4261 4 paper
A special issue of The Journal of Legislative Studies

FRANK CASS PUBLISHERS
Newbury House, 900 Eastern Avenue, Newbury Park, Ilford, Essex IG2 7HH
Tel: +44 (0)181 599 8866 Fax: +44 (0)181 599 0984 E-mail: info@frankcass.com
NORTH AMERICA
c/o ISBS, 5804 NE Hassalo Street, Portland, OR 97213 3644, USA
Tel: 1 800 944 6190 Fax: 503 280 8832 E-mail cass@isbs.com
Website: http://www.frankcass.com

Members of Parliament in Western Europe
Roles and Behaviour

Wolfgang C. Müller, *University of Vienna* and
Thomas Saalfeld, *University of Kent* (Eds)

Traditional comparative studies of parliaments have focused on constitutional and organisational characteristics of parliaments, or differences in the historical contexts, in which legislative assemblies have developed. This volume provides empirical work on legislative role orientations and behaviour in Belgium, Denmark, Germany, the Netherlands, Norway and the United Kingdom.

176 pages 1997
0 7146 4821 3 cloth   0 7146 4369 6 paper
A special issue of The Journal of Legislative Studies

Parliaments in Western Europe

Philip Norton, *University of Hull* (Ed)
With new preface

> *'An excellent little book. In its compressed format, it succeeds in providing highly relevant, often quantitative, up-to-date information on institutional and behavioural developments in seven Western European Parliaments'*
> **Government & Opposition**

This book provides the first contemporary analysis of the various parliaments in western Europe. Each author addresses two central questions: to what extext has the legislature been marginalised in policy-making, and to what extent has it been able to maintain popular support?

176 pages   1990   2nd Edition 1996   0 7146 4331 9 paper

FRANK CASS PUBISHERS
Newbury House, 900 Eastern Avenue, Newbury Park, Ilford, Essex IG2 7HH
Tel: +44 (0)181 599 8866 Fax: +44 (0)181 599 0984 E-mail: info@frankcass.com
NORTH AMERICA
c/o ISBS, 5804 NE Hassalo Street, Portland, OR 97213 3644, USA
Tel: 1 800 944 6190 Fax: 503 280 8832 E-mail cass@isbs.com
Website: http://www.frankcass.com